# THE ART OF
# BLACKWORK
# EMBROIDERY

# THE ART OF BLACKWORK EMBROIDERY

Rosemary Drysdale

CHARLES SCRIBNER'S SONS NEW YORK

Library of Congress Cataloging in Publication Data

Drysdale, Rosemary.
    The art of blackwork embroidery.
        1.  Blackwork embroidery.  I.  Title.
TT778.B5D79        746.4′4        75-6990
ISBN 0-684-14330-5

1 3 5 7 9 11 13 15 17 19 MD/C 20 18 16 14 12 10 8 6 4 2

PRINTED IN THE UNITED STATES OF AMERICA

FRONTIS:
Blackwork sampler of the 1930's. (*Collection of the Embroiderer's Guild*)

# CONTENTS

# THE ART OF
# BLACKWORK
# EMBROIDERY

# INTRODUCTION

THIS book has been designed to teach you an elegant but simple form of embroidery, blackwork, and also to show you how easy it is to plan and execute your own designs.

All the designs in this book are worked by counting the threads. For the beginner the counted-thread technique is by far the simplest form of embroidery, because all you do is fill geometric shapes with a pattern of stitchery. There is no end to the variety of patterns you can create or to the different effects that may be achieved by the choice of fabric and yarn.

The counted-thread technique is the embroidering of simple stitches over an equal number of threads. When worked in black yarn on white fabric it is known as blackwork.

Blackwork embroidery is an art dating as far back as the fourteenth century. In Chaucer's *Canterbury Tales* the carpenter's wife in the "Miller's Tale" is quoted as wearing a blackwork smock and cap:

White was her smock, embroidered all before and even behind, her collar round about. Of coal-black silk, on both sides, in and out; The strings of the white cap upon her head Were, like her collar, black silk worked with thread . . .

However, blackwork really became popular in England when Henry VIII married Catherine of Aragon in 1509. The Spanish Catherine was an enthusiastic embroiderer and converted the ladies of her court to this new and stylish stitchery.

As blackwork embroidery patterns resemble lace (which was difficult to obtain in Tudor days, because of a tax on lace) collars and cuffs of blackwork embroidery soon appeared on the courtiers' clothing. These collars and cuffs had to be equally beautiful on both sides of the material, as both the back and front were visible. Holbein stitch, which is identical on both sides, developed out of this necessity. The name Holbein was taken from Hans Holbein, who for a long time worked as portrait painter at the English Court. Some of Holbein's portraits show Henry VIII and others adorned with embroidery, hence the name Holbein Stitch.

OPPOSITE:

A painting by Hans Holbein of Henry VIII, age 49. Henry's sleeves are adorned with blackwork patterns. (*Courtesy Galleria Nazionale d'Arte Antica—Palazzo Barberini-Roma*)

ANNO · ÆTATIS · · SVÆ · X

Man's night cap. Linen embroidered with black silver and gilt thread. English; late 16th Century. (*Courtesy of the Victoria and Albert Museum.* Crown copyright)

Blackwork was sometimes given a more elaborate effect by enhancing the work with touches of silver and gold threads.

The painting of the Virgin and Saint Anne by Francisco de Zurbarán in 1655, shows both the Virgin and Saint Anne embroidering.

The Virgin's piece can be identified as blackwork. This painting is on display in the Metropolitan Museum of Art in New York City.

Blackwork embroidery remained popular in England until the late seventeenth century. As subsequent fashions changed, little blackwork was to be found. However, touches continued to appear on clothing, samplers, and occasionally on household and bed linens.

With today's revived interest in crafts, blackwork embroidery is again appearing. Magazine articles are mentioning blackwork and embroidered pieces appear in homes and on clothing.

Triangular forehead cloth. Linen embroidered with black silk. English; early 17th Century. (*Courtesy of the Victoria and Albert Museum*. Crown copyright)

Once more blackwork is alive. I am sure you will have fun looking for blackwork pieces, examining paintings and old samplers, and discovering how many blackwork patterns you can find and easily adapt to today's fashions.

# LEARNING
# BLACKWORK
# EMBROIDERY

ALL you need to master is counting the fabric threads and working the simple straight-line stitches.

Blackwork embroidery is the application of simple straight-line stitches to form basic patterns and then the repetition of these patterns to create a finished design. The effect of the work is achieved by the complexity of each pattern. A close pattern will produce a dark effect and an open pattern a light effect.

Although the completed designs are rich in appearance and can be marvelously sophisticated, blackwork is actually very simple. The basic principle is a series of single straight lines (stitched threads)

A close pattern produces a dark effect.

An open pattern produces a light effect.

joined to form a pattern. The design grows out of the repetition of these pattern units.

One of the pleasures of doing blackwork is the joy of seeing *your* pattern grow on a once-blank piece of fabric. Once begun it is difficult to put down the piece until it is complete. And when it is complete, and draws admiring comments, you'll be especially satisfied to know you created it yourself.

The distinction between blackwork embroidery and most other popular embroidery is that rather than stitching from someone else's drawing you are learning to create your own designs.

## THE STITCHES

Various patterns are used in blackwork embroidery. All these patterns are based on straight stitches, which are the following:

1. Back Stitch
2. Double Running Stitch (sometimes called Holbein Stitch)
3. Cross Stitch and its variations

Before you begin your first piece of blackwork, practice these stitches on your sampler until you are completely at ease with them. (See page 35, "Your Sampler.")

### *BACK STITCH*

Each stitch is the same number of threads long. The stitch is worked from A back to B and forward to C. The effect achieved is a solid, unbroken line (Figure 1).

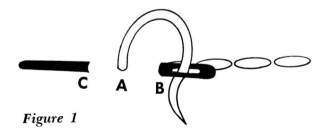

C   A   B

*Figure 1*

## DOUBLE RUNNING OR HOLBEIN STITCH

Come up at A and down at B and up again at C (Figure 2a). A B is the same number of threads as B C—for example, over 4 threads, under 4 threads, over 4 threads. Work a row.

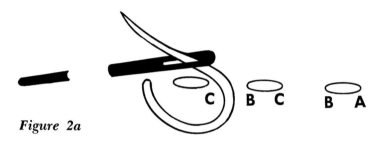

*Figure 2a*

Turn the work around and fill in the spaces, going into the same holes made by the first row of running stitches (Figure 2b). This stitch forms a continuous line exactly alike on both sides, and therefore reversible.

*Figure 2b*

On the diagram, the second row of stitches is shown in a darker color of yarn. This is to show it clearer. When working, work both rows in the same color.

## CROSS STITCH

Come up at A, down at B, and up at C.

A to B is the same number of threads up and over—for example, up at A count 4 threads up and 4 threads to the left and down at B. Then count 4 threads down and up at C (Figure 3a).

Now go down at D 4 threads to the right of B (Figure 3b).

Note: Always make the top diagonal stitch of the crosses slope in the same direction throughout the pattern.

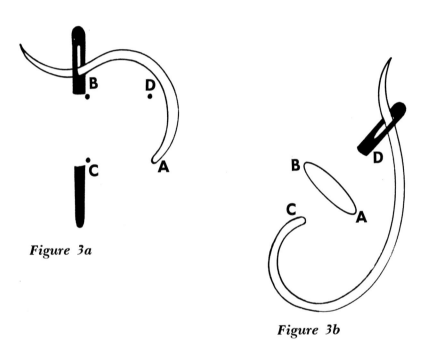

Figure 3a

Figure 3b

A single Cross Stitch

## *REVERSIBLE CROSS STITCH*

Come up at A, down at B, and up at C. Continue in this way, making a row of slanted stitches. The dotted line shows how the stitch will appear on the reverse side of the fabric (Figure 4a).

Next, work back along the row crossing over the slanted stitches.

An equal work space is formed between each Cross Stitch (Figure 4b). In these spaces repeat the above steps, filling in the spaces (Figures c and d). The Cross stitches formed are completely reversible.

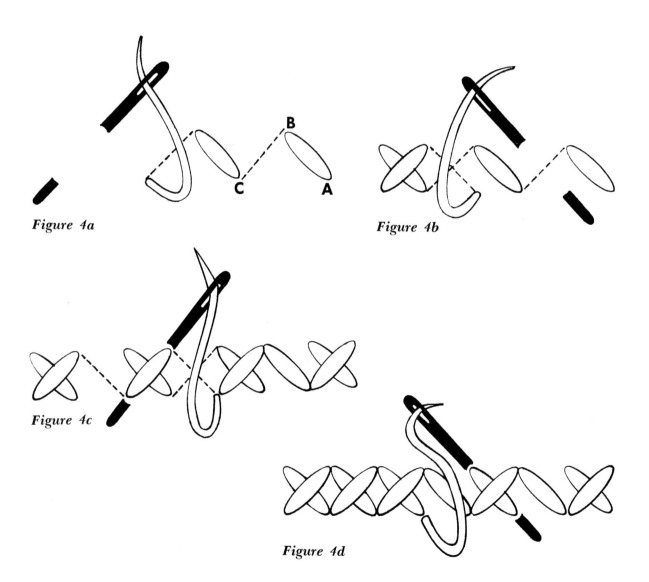

*Figure 4a*

*Figure 4b*

*Figure 4c*

*Figure 4d*

## *EYE STITCH*

This stitch is made up of eight straight stitches all of equal length and radiating from a central point. The finished result should form a square (Figures 5a, b, and c).

A small hole will form in the center of the stitch.

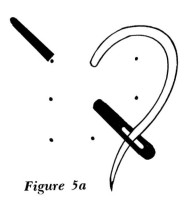

**Figure 5a**

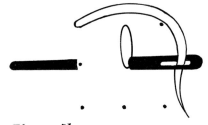

**Figure 5b**

**Figure 5c**

## DOUBLE CROSS STITCH

Work a simple Cross, then come up at E, halfway between B and C (Figure 6a).

Go down at F, halfway between A and D, and up at G, halfway between A and C (Figure 6b).

Finally go down at H, halfway between B and D (Figure 6c).

This stitch is different from the Eye Stitch, because it does not radiate from a central point (Figure 6d).

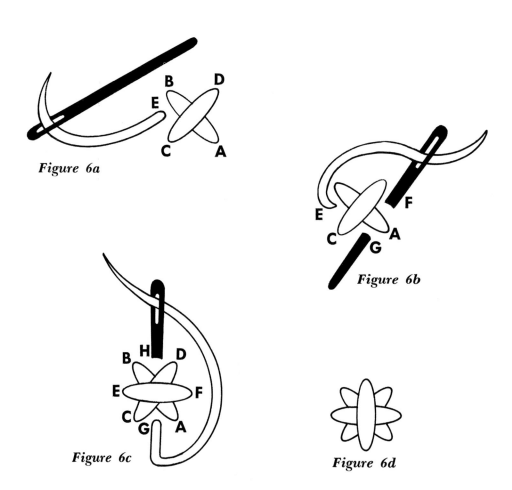

*Figure 6a*

*Figure 6b*

*Figure 6c*

*Figure 6d*

# PATTERN DARNING

Pattern darning is Running Stitch worked in and out of the fabric threads to make various patterns. The different patterns are made by the number of threads picked up or passed over (see photographs).

Pattern darning. Running stitches worked horizontally in various patterns.

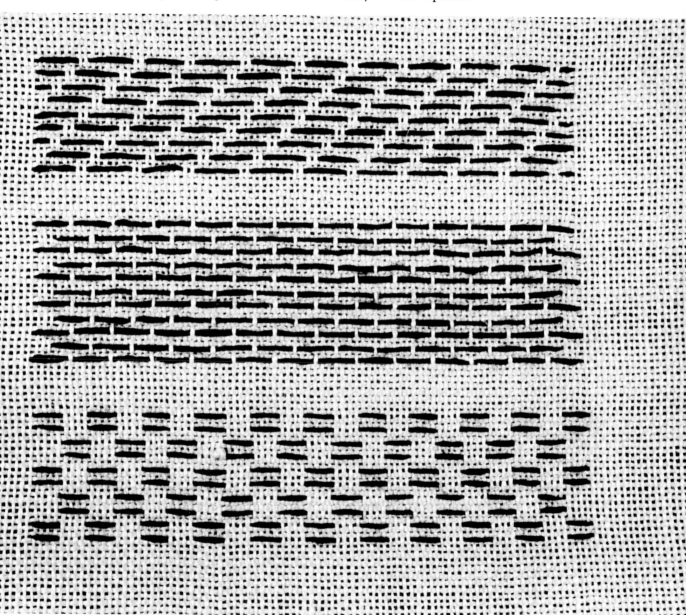

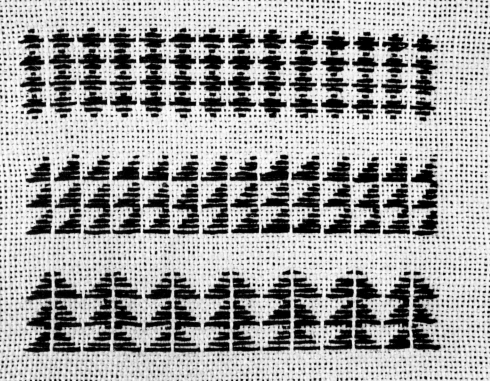

Pattern Darning. Running stitches worked closer together making more solid patterns.

Pattern Darning. Running stitches worked vertically.

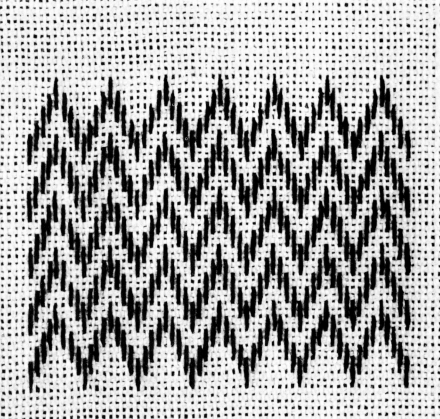

## THREADING THE NEEDLE

Whenever possible, always thread the needle BEFORE cutting the yarn from the bobbin. By doing this the rub of the thread is down and this prevents knotting or fraying.

Another method of preventing the thread from knotting or fraying is to work with only 18″ of thread at a time. If it is any longer, the thread may begin to wear and produce a smudged, fluffy appearance.

## STARTING A STITCH

As the weave of the appropriate fabric is fairly loose, do not use a knot to begin a stitch, because it will slip out of the holes of the weave. Instead, a thread of about 4″ should be left hanging on the back of the design. Work 6 stitches and then, with another needle, the 4″ thread should be darned or whipped into the backs of the already worked stitches. This will hold the thread and prevent the stitches from unraveling (Figure 7).

**Starting a stitch**

*Figure 7*

## ENDING A STITCH

Always leave sufficient thread in the needle to finish off the work securely (6″ is usually sufficient).

Take the working thread onto the back of the design and weave it into the previously worked stitches. Remember to work over the same place a few times at intervals to ensure it is secure (Figure 8).

**Ending a stitch**

*Figure 8*

# THE MATERIALS
# NEEDED TO
# DO BLACKWORK

BLACKWORK embroidery is an art, and as an art it should be cherished. We are able to see fine samples of sixteenth-century blackwork today because of the excellent quality of the materials used in the past. First-quality materials should be used to ensure the pieces you create will last for generations.

## FABRICS

Any fabric you choose must have an even weave with round, well-spaced threads. The threads should be thick enough to count accurately. An even weave is one that has the same number of warp threads as weft threads to the inch (see photograph below).

The more threads woven to the inch, the finer the fabric, and therefore, the finer the embroidery.

A suitable weave is 22 threads to the square inch.

Close up of an even weave linen fabric showing 22 threads to the inch.

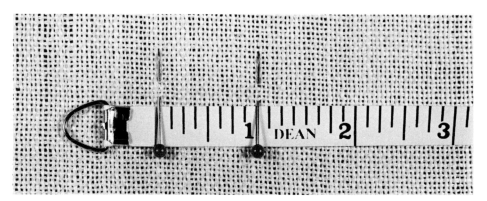

Linen fabrics are the strongest and wear the best and are therefore the most suitable for blackwork embroidery.

Other suitable fabrics are:

Even, loose-weave cotton
Even-weave synthetic fabrics

I find that for pillows, small wall hangings, and any smaller pieces a 100 percent even-weave linen table napkin is excellent. Most of the samples in this book are worked on linen table napkins. These napkins are available in various colors and weights and can be purchased in all large department stores.

Fine, medium and coarse linen even weave fabrics.

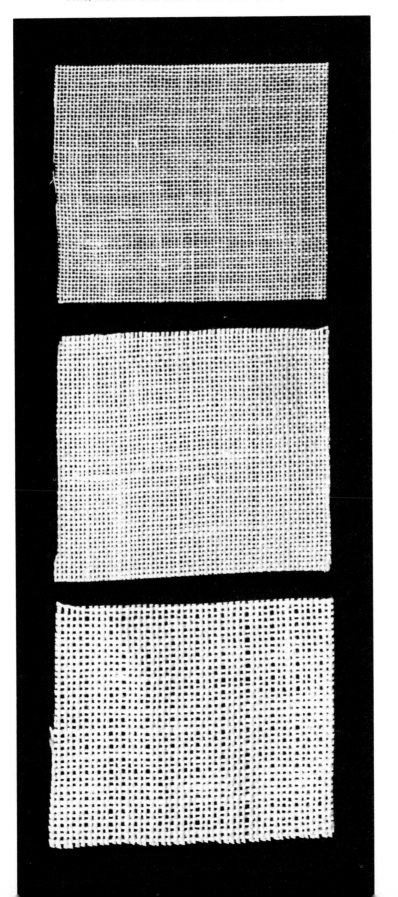

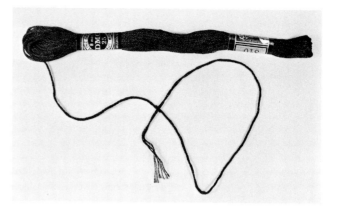

A skein of stranded floss with the strands separated to show the 6 individual strands.

# YARNS

Here again, good quality is essential. The weight of the yarn chosen should correspond to the weight of the fabric threads to be stitched. Stranded floss is ideal, because it can be used in either one or more strands to achieve any desired effect (see photograph).

Other suitable yarns are:

D.M.C. Linen Thread (available in various weights)
D.M.C. Cotton Perle
Fine crocheting cottons and linens
Silver and gold threads (D.M.C. Fil D'orà Broder)

Various yarns suitable for blackwork.

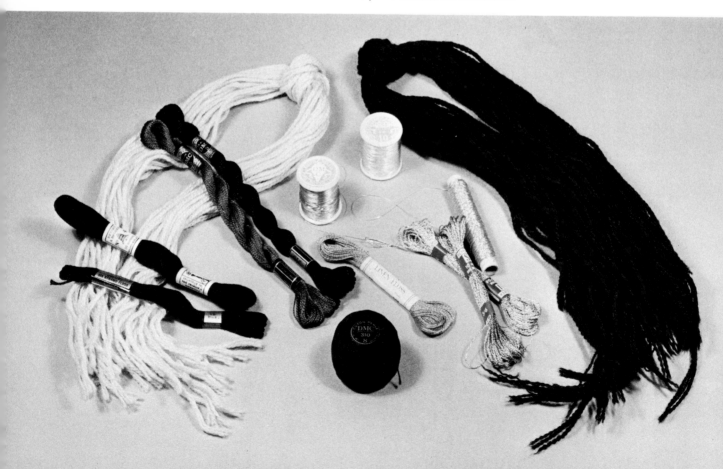

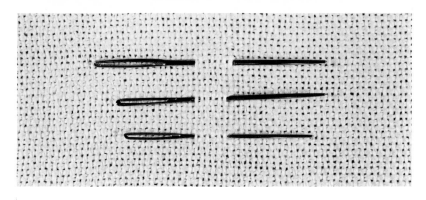

Tapestry needles. Notice the blunt ends and large eyes.

## THE NEEDLES

Needles without points (such as tapestry needles) are best, because their blunt ends are able to slip between the weave of the fabric without splitting the threads.

The eye of the needle should be large enough to take the embroidery yarn without rubbing, to ensure against fraying.

Tapestry needles are sold by size. A #24 needle is suitable for a fine thread and a #22 for a coarser thread.

## A FRAME

An embroidery frame can be used to help hold the fabric taut, and keep the weave threads straight. With the use of the frame, the threads will be easier to count.

A square frame.

A square type of frame is most suitable. With the square frame all the fabric to be embroidered is visible and taut. However, a perfect piece of blackwork can be created without the use of any frame.

As a rule, a square frame is more suitable for the larger pieces of work, while smaller pieces can be worked beautifully in the hand. The samples in this book were executed without a frame.

## YOUR WORKBAG

A workbag or basket in which to keep your materials is essential. Along with the project you are embroidering, you should carry a pair of sharp-pointed embroidery scissors, a tape measure, pins, basting thread, a thimble (if you use one), and a pad of graph paper.

An assortment of the materials you will need.

Buy the thickest pad of graph paper you can find—you will be amazed at how often you will use it to work out new ideas and jot down patterns you see.

Early 17th century sampler showing Holbein Work. (*Courtesy of the Victoria and Albert Museum.* Crown copyright)

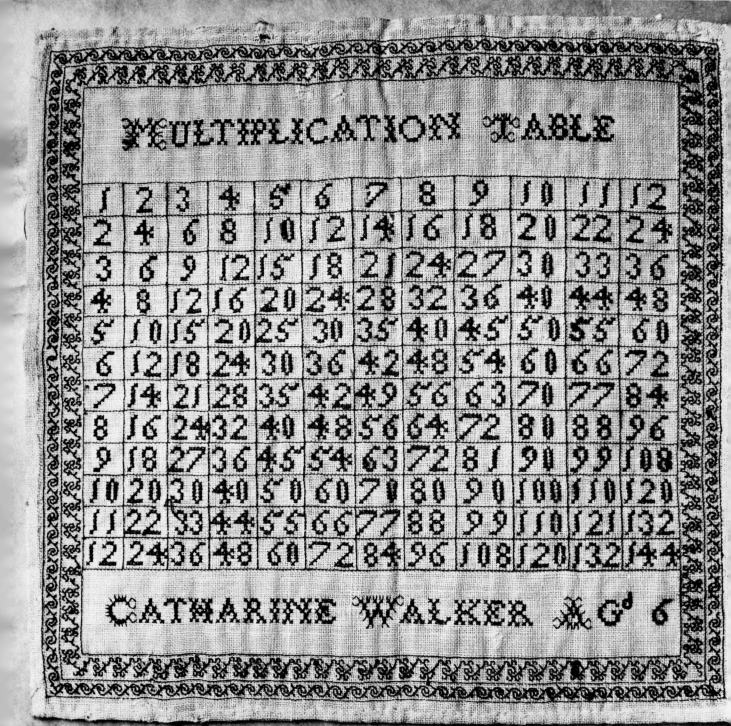

## MULTIPLICATION TABLE

| 1 | 2 | 3 | 4 | 5 | 6 | 7 | 8 | 9 | 10 | 11 | 12 |
|---|---|---|---|---|---|---|---|---|---|---|---|
| 2 | 4 | 6 | 8 | 10 | 12 | 14 | 16 | 18 | 20 | 22 | 24 |
| 3 | 6 | 9 | 12 | 15 | 18 | 21 | 24 | 27 | 30 | 33 | 36 |
| 4 | 8 | 12 | 16 | 20 | 24 | 28 | 32 | 36 | 40 | 44 | 48 |
| 5 | 10 | 15 | 20 | 25 | 30 | 35 | 40 | 45 | 50 | 55 | 60 |
| 6 | 12 | 18 | 24 | 30 | 36 | 42 | 48 | 54 | 60 | 66 | 72 |
| 7 | 14 | 21 | 28 | 35 | 42 | 49 | 56 | 63 | 70 | 77 | 84 |
| 8 | 16 | 24 | 32 | 40 | 48 | 56 | 64 | 72 | 80 | 88 | 96 |
| 9 | 18 | 27 | 36 | 45 | 54 | 63 | 72 | 81 | 90 | 99 | 108 |
| 10 | 20 | 30 | 40 | 50 | 60 | 70 | 80 | 90 | 100 | 110 | 120 |
| 11 | 22 | 33 | 44 | 55 | 66 | 77 | 88 | 99 | 110 | 121 | 132 |
| 12 | 24 | 36 | 48 | 60 | 72 | 84 | 96 | 108 | 120 | 132 | 144 |

## CATHARINE WALKER AG^d 6

Child's multiplication table sampler worked in Black Cross Stitch and Double Running Stitch by Catherine Walker, aged 6 years. On display at Blair Castle, Scotland. (*By permission of His Grace the Duke of Atholl.*)

## THE SAMPLER

In its origin a sampler was an example (sample) of stitches used in embroidery. Because of the scarcity of pattern books the embroiderer copied down on fabric any stitches or patterns she wanted to keep. In this way the sampler developed.

In Britain during the fifteenth to seventeenth centuries the popularity of embroidery grew. The sampler itself became one of the most popular forms of needlework.

Blackwork embroidery patterns appeared on the samplers of the sixteenth century and their stitches and patterns have remained popular on samplers to the present day.

## YOUR SAMPLER

It is very important that you have a sampler to practice the stitches in this book and to record other patterns you find attractive.

To make a sampler all you need are the following:

1. A piece of even-weave fabric with approximately 22 threads to the inch (22 threads is suggested because all the stitched patterns in this book are worked on 22 threads per inch)
2. Black embroidery thread (6-strand floss)
3. A #22 tapestry needle

Any time you are planning a design on a different weave of fabric or using a yarn other than the embroidery floss, always make a new sampler in the same fabric and yarn as the piece to be worked on. On your sampler practice the stitches and pattern effects you will be using. DO NOT bother to rip out mistakes. Instead, move over to a new area and begin again. Time is too precious to waste ripping out work. If all your mistakes can be made on your sampler, you should be able to work error-free on your finished piece.

Always have your sampler or samplers on hand for reference and experiment.

I made a sampler into a workbag and in this way I always have many useful patterns worked out in front of me. Inside my bag, along with the piece of embroidery I am working on, I also carry the appropriate sampler.

Blackwork sampler made up into a work bag.

# STARTING A
# PROJECT

YOU are now ready to make your first piece of blackwork.

The following instructions show you, step by step, the making of a 14″ x 14″ white linen blackwork pillow.

Follow these instructions and you will be thrilled with the finished result.

(Read the complete instructions before beginning the steps.)

Blackwork pillow.

# MATERIALS

2 pieces of white even-weave linen, 16″ x 16″ (22 threads per inch), or 2 white linen table napkins

2 skeins of black embroidery floss

Tapestry needle size 22

1¾ yard of 2″ wide white eyelet ribbon (can be omitted if a knife-edge pillow is to be made)

Colored basting thread

### Step 1

Cut two pieces of even-weave fabric 16″ x 16″ or use a linen table napkin of approximately 15¾″ x 15¾″. The weave should have 22 threads to the inch.

### Step 2

Either tape the raw edges of the fabric with masking tape, over sew them with a basting thread, or turn over a single hem and baste. (This step is very important as it prevents the fabric from unraveling.) When using a table napkin omit this step (see photograph and Figure 9a, b, and c).

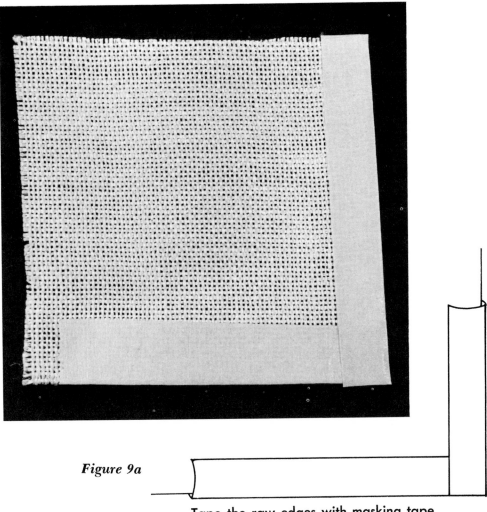

*Figure 9a*

Tape the raw edges with masking tape.

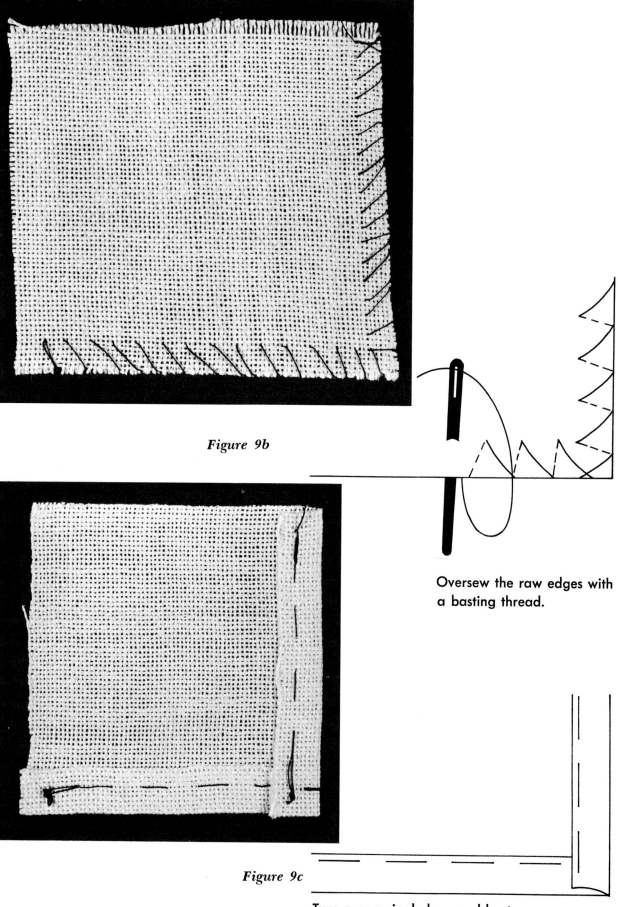

*Figure 9b*

Oversew the raw edges with
a basting thread.

*Figure 9c*

Turn over a single hem and baste.

*Step 3*

## *MAKING A FRAMEWORK FOR THE DESIGN*

It is important to mark the center point, as most of the patterns in this book are worked starting at the center point.

    A. Finding the center point

      1. Using one of the 16″ x 16″ pieces of fabric, fold it in half lengthwise.
      2. Baste along the fold with a colored basting thread.
      3. Fold the fabric in half widthwise.
      4. Baste along the fold with a colored basting thread.
      5. The place where the basting threads cross is the center point (see Figure 10).

NOTE: The basting threads are stitched in between the fabric threads (see photograph, page 42).

*Figure 10*

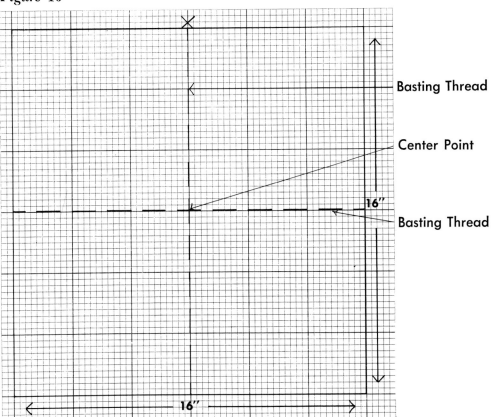

Basting Thread

Center Point

16″

Basting Thread

16″

The basting threads are stitched in between the fabric threads.

B. Marking the design area

Count from the center point 66 threads to the left, and 66 threads to the right. Stitch a basting thread down either side. Then

*Figure 11*

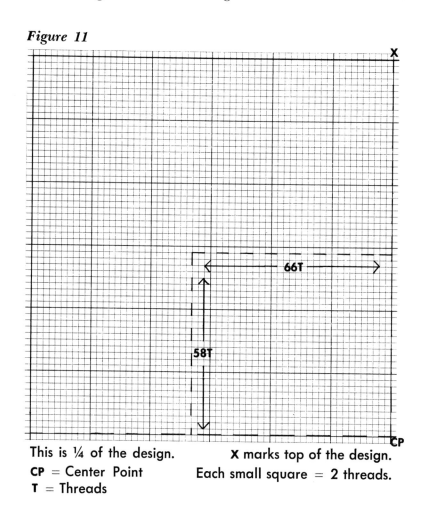

This is ¼ of the design.     **X** marks top of the design.
**CP** = Center Point     Each small square = 2 threads.
**T** = Threads

count 58 threads above the center point and 58 threads below. Stitch a basting thread above and below.

A square is now made measuring approximately 6¼″ wide and 5½″ high (see Figure 11).

C. Marking the Border Area

Count 20 threads to each side of the design area and baste another square. Then count 12 threads from this line and baste a second square.

Finally, baste a square 7″ from either side and top and bottom of the center point. This marks the stitching area for the finished pillow. An X can be stitched to show the top of the pillow (see Figure 12). The fabric is now perfectly charted for you to begin to embroider.

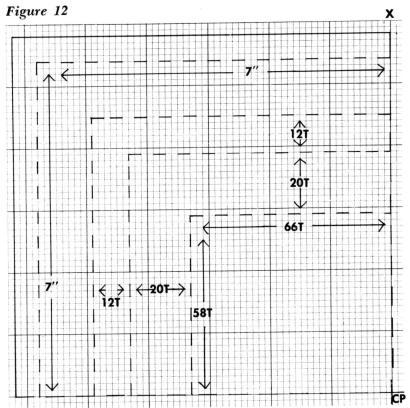

Figure 12

This is ¼ of the design area.
**CP** = Center Point
**T** = Threads
**X** marks top of the design.
Each small square = 2 threads.

### Step 4

On your sampler, practice the Double Running Stitch and pattern number 34, using 2 strands of embroidery floss.

All the stitches are worked over 4 threads of the fabric.

### Step 5

Begin at the center point of pattern number 34 and work a Cross Stitch over 4 threads of the fabric.

The center basting lines will run in the middle of the Cross Stitch (see Figure 13).

Use two strands of the embroidery floss.

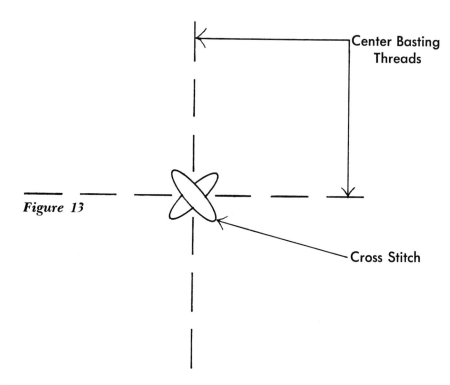

**Figure 13**

### Step 6

Work the pattern as shown in Figures 14a, b, c, d and e, working 56 square motifs in all.

*Figure 14*

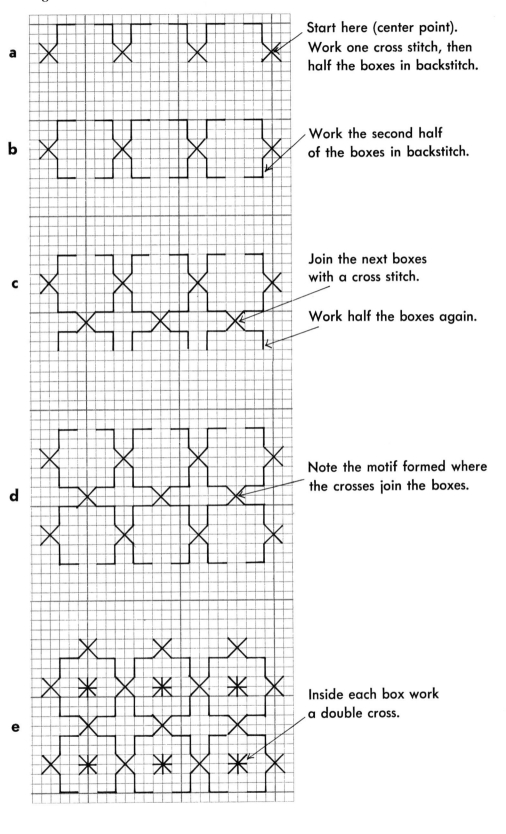

**a** — Start here (center point). Work one cross stitch, then half the boxes in backstitch.

**b** — Work the second half of the boxes in backstitch.

**c** — Join the next boxes with a cross stitch.

Work half the boxes again.

**d** — Note the motif formed where the crosses join the boxes.

**e** — Inside each box work a double cross.

*Step 7*

Work the first row of the border in Double Running Stitch (over 4 threads and under 4 threads) 20 threads from the basting line of the design area. Work the second row of double-running stitches 12 threads from the first row (Figure 15).

The basting threads mark the area clearly.

## Step 8

Inside the border work the Double Cross Stitch 4 threads apart starting at point A, as shown in Figure 15.

*Figure 15*

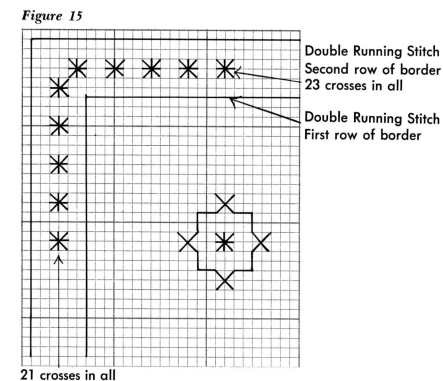

Double Running Stitch
Second row of border
23 crosses in all

Double Running Stitch
First row of border

21 crosses in all

Each small square = 2 threads

Work 21 crosses on the right and left side of the border and 23 crosses on the top and bottom of the border.

### Step 9. Making Up the Pillow

A. Press the finished piece. To do this first lay the embroidery right side down on a terry towel, then, using a hot iron and a wet

*Figure 16*

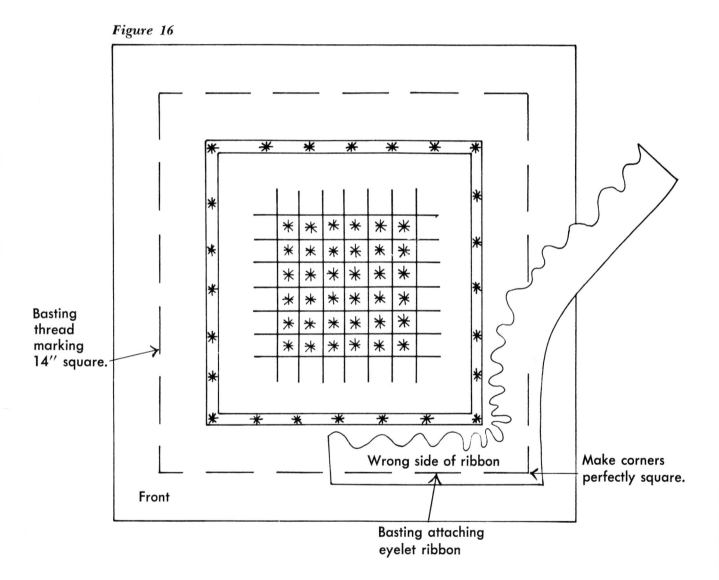

Basting thread marking 14″ square.

Front

Wrong side of ribbon

Make corners perfectly square.

Basting attaching eyelet ribbon

pressing cloth, press the embroidery flat and square. Allow the piece to dry.

B. With the embroidered side uppermost, baste the eyelet ribbon along the 14″ square marked by the basting thread. Be sure to place the lace edge of the ribbon toward the center of the work. (This is clearly shown in Figure 16.) Then machine or hand-stitch the lace in place. (If a knife-edge pillow without the lace trim is being made, omit this step.)

C. Place pillow back over the embroidery and lace, right sides together, and baste along the same 14″ square (3 layers in all, see Figure 17 ).

*Figure 17*

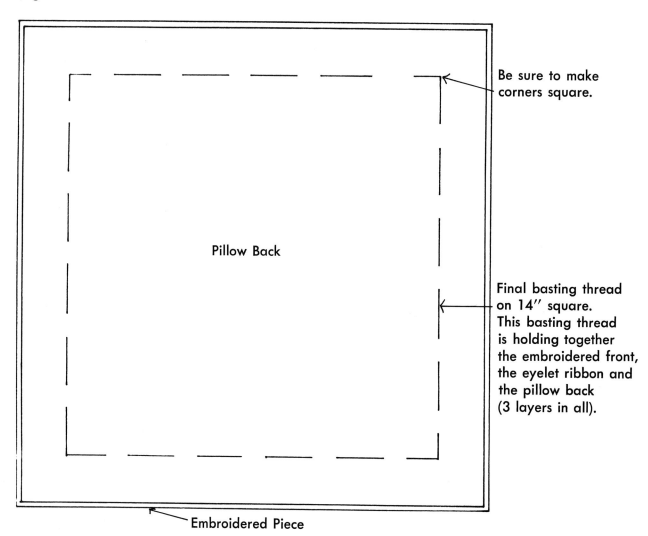

Be sure to make corners square.

Pillow Back

Final basting thread on 14″ square. This basting thread is holding together the embroidered front, the eyelet ribbon and the pillow back (3 layers in all).

Embroidered Piece

D. Next, machine-stitch, or using tiny Back stitches, hand-sew around three sides and 1″ in on either side of the fourth side. Be sure to make the corners square. Remove basting threads (see Figure 18).

E. Trim excess fabric away to ½″ from the stitching.

*Figure 18*

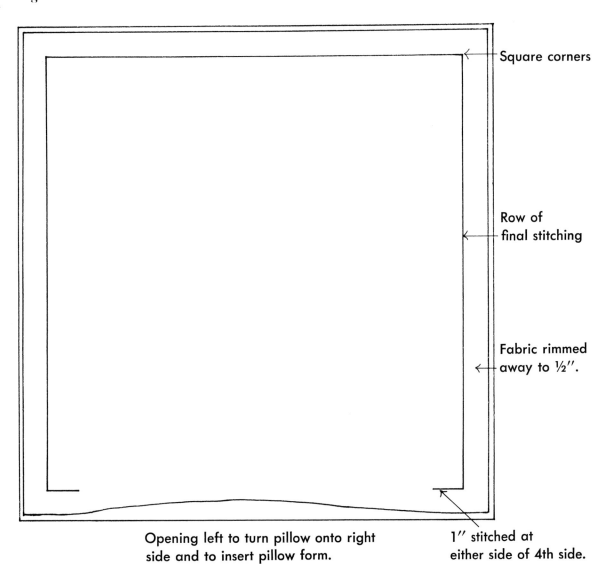

Square corners

Row of final stitching

Fabric rimmed away to ½″.

Opening left to turn pillow onto right side and to insert pillow form.

1″ stitched at either side of 4th side.

F. Turn the embroidery to the right side, square out the corners.

G. Fill with a 14″ x 14″ inner pillow form of a good-quality material such as foam or Dacron.

H. Hand-sew the fourth side closed (see Figure 19).

**Figure 19**

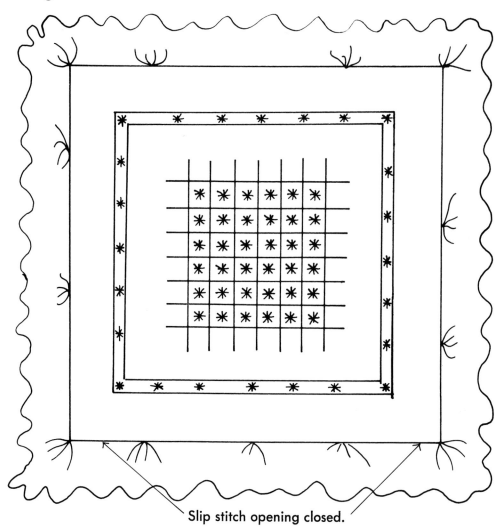

Slip stitch opening closed.

# THE PATTERNS

ON the graphs each square represents two threads of the fabric. The arrows mark the center point of some patterns. On other patterns select a Cross Stitch or single motif (for example, Eye Stitch) as the center point.

51

## DARK PATTERNS

# Pattern No. 1

This is a very simple pattern, giving a very dark effect. It is formed by working a Double Cross Stitch and then a single Cross Stitch alternately.

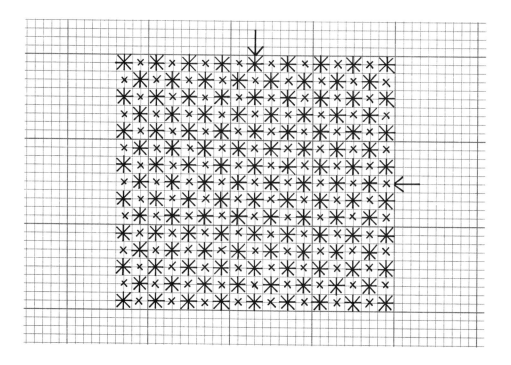

# Pattern No. 2

If this pattern is worked in Back Stitch, a series of straight lines is formed on the wrong side of the fabric. For a reversible effect, use Double Running Stitch.

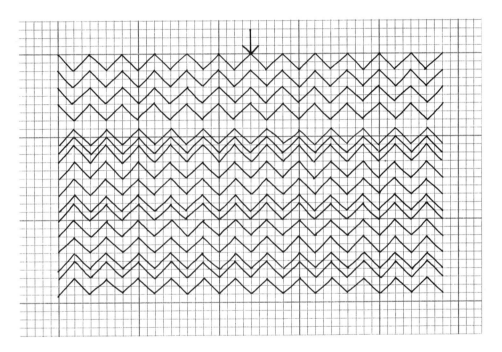

# Pattern No. 3

This beautiful pattern is worked radiating from the center of the shape outward (Figure a). A hole is formed in the center of each star.

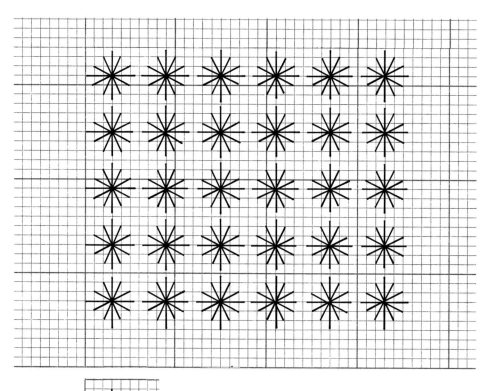

 *Figure a*

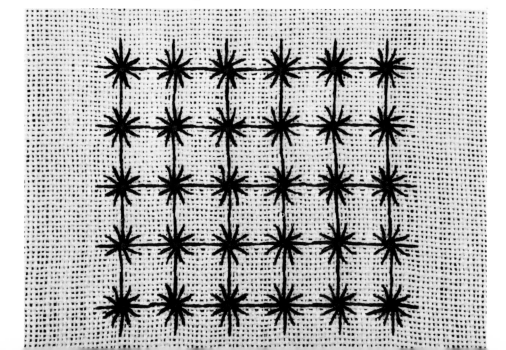

# Pattern No. 4

This is a very dark pattern resembling flowers or foliage. A hole is formed at the base of each motif. The longest stitch is worked over 8 threads (Figure a).

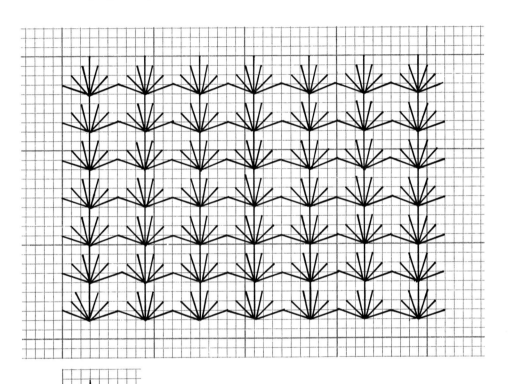

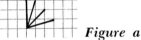
*Figure a*

# Pattern No. 5

A dark, all-over effect is achieved with this pattern. First work all the Cross stitches over 4 threads (Figure a), then on every alternate row enclose the crosses in boxes (Figure b.)

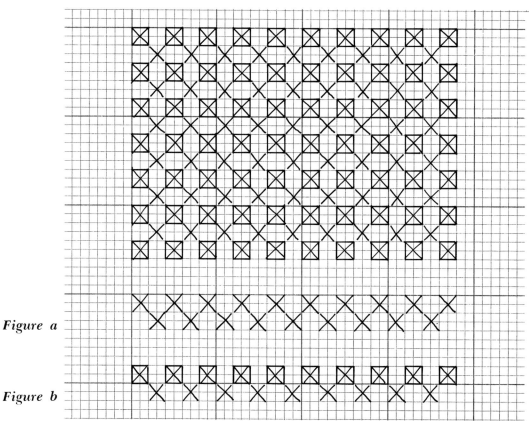

*Figure a*

*Figure b*

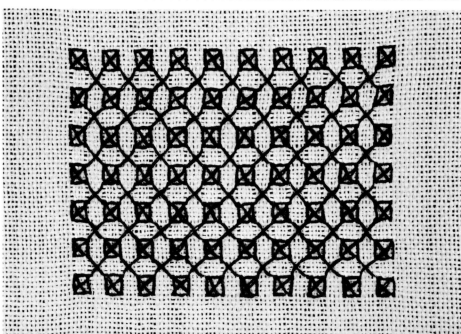

# Pattern No. 6

Although similar to Pattern #5, this gives a lighter effect. First work the boxes 4 threads apart, then join them together, alternating a Double Cross Stitch with a single Cross Stitch. A very useful pattern.

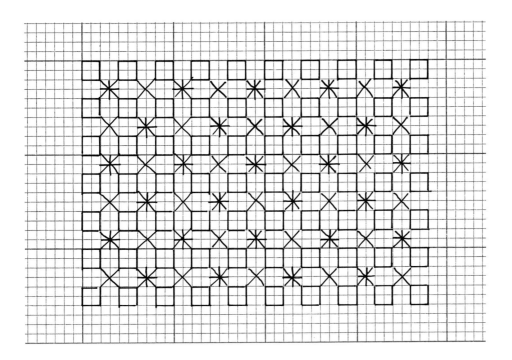

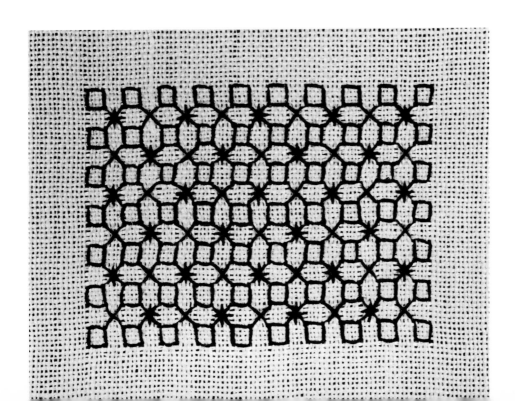

# Pattern No. 7

This pattern resembles a spider web and needs a fairly large area to be seen at its best. A hole is formed in the center of each unit.

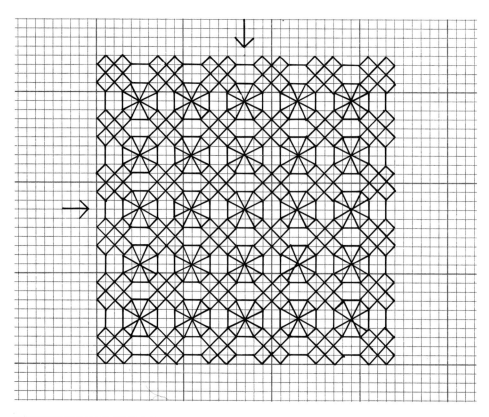

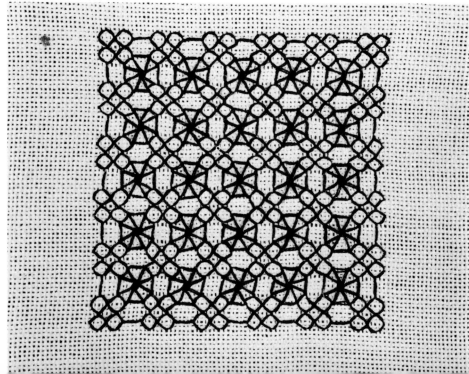

# Pattern No. 8

This is a very easy pattern to stitch, producing a lovely delicate design, suitable for small pieces. The stitches are worked over 2 threads, using the Back Stitch and Cross Stitch.

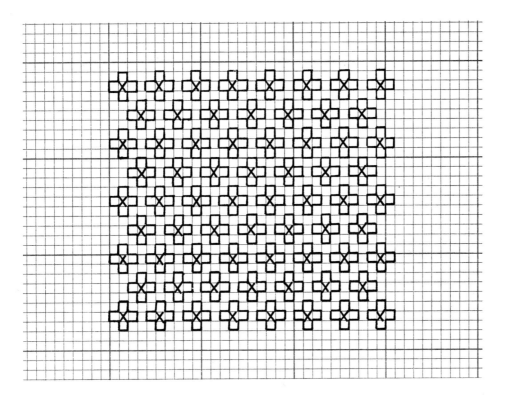

# Pattern No. 9

A very dark pattern forming a leaflike motif. The straight stitches forming the "leaves" are worked first (Figure a) and then joined together with Cross stitches.

*Figure a*

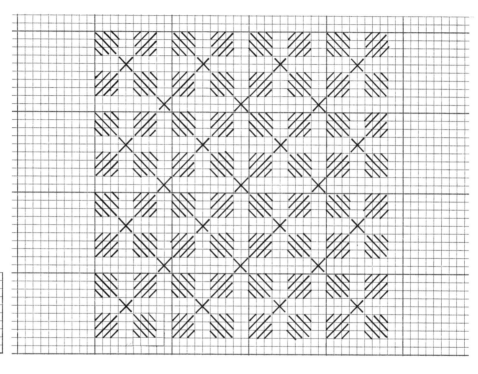

# Pattern No. 10

A floral pattern requiring a large area to be appreciated. The four quarters of the motif are joined together by a Cross Stitch. The longest stitches are worked over 6 threads.

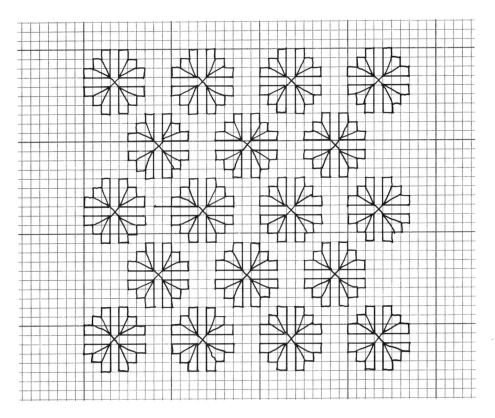

# Pattern No. 11

This pattern can be used either vertically or horizontally. It is worked in Back Stitch, with a straight Cross Stitch worked in the center of every alternate row. Straight lines are formed on the wrong side of the work.

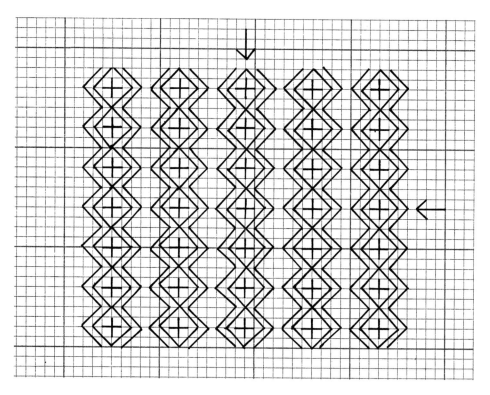

# Pattern No. 12

Although simple, this delicate pattern takes concentration. Work the motif in Figure a and then work a Cross Stitch over its center (Figure b).

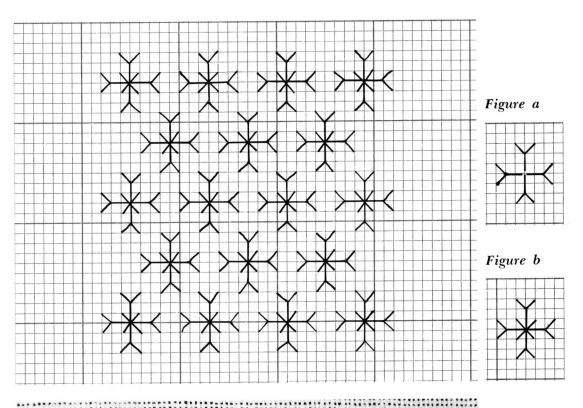

*Figure a*

*Figure b*

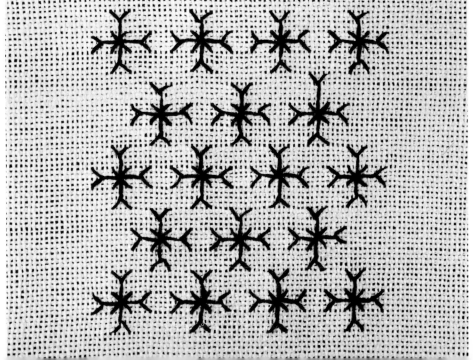

# Pattern No. 13

This is a very ornate pattern worked in Back Stitch over two threads. When all the Back Stitch motifs are worked the spaces left are each connected with 16 straight stitches radiating from a central point, and worked over 7 threads. This is one of my favorites.

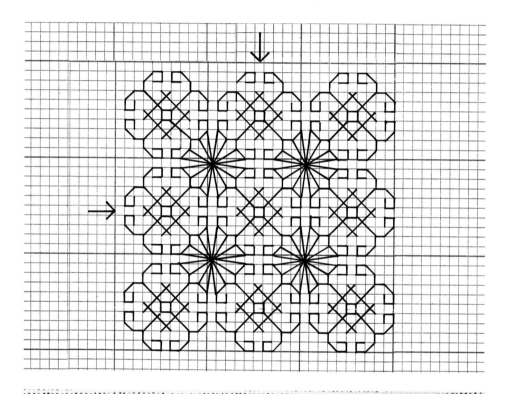

# Pattern No. 14

A very heavy pattern producing an all-over dark effect. First work the Cross stitches diagonally over four threads (Figure a). Next enclose each Cross Stitch in a box using the Back Stitch. These stitches are worked into the same holes as the Cross stitches (Figure b). In the shape left, work 8 straight stitches radiating from the center and touching the point of the eight squares (Figure c). The pattern can also be used as a single motif (Figure d), or, omitting the straight stitches, used as a border (Figure e).

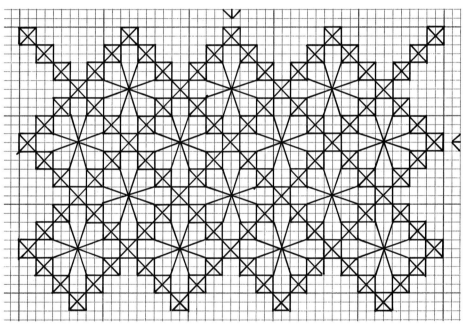

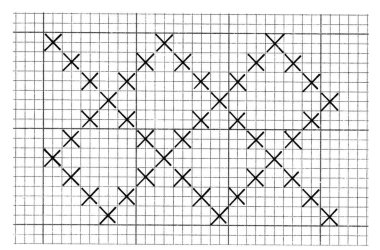

*Figure a*

*Figure b*

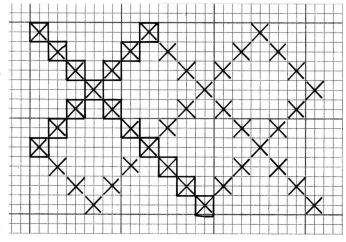

*Figure c*

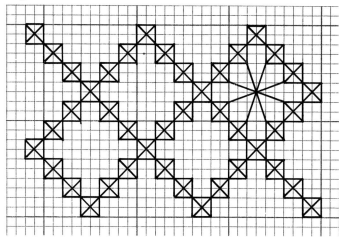

*Figure d*

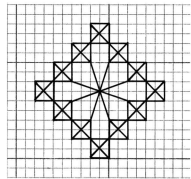

*Figure e*

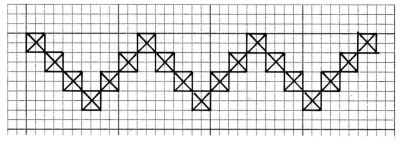

# Pattern No. 15

This is a very beautiful pattern, which appears complicated, but is simple to stitch. The main pattern is worked in Back Stitch over 2 threads of the fabric. Work the flower motifs first (Figure a). The star inside of each flower is worked in Eye Stitch over 2 threads. In the squares left work the motif shown in Figure b. The straight lines are worked over 3 threads and the diagonals over 4 threads. The tiny square in the center is 2 threads square.

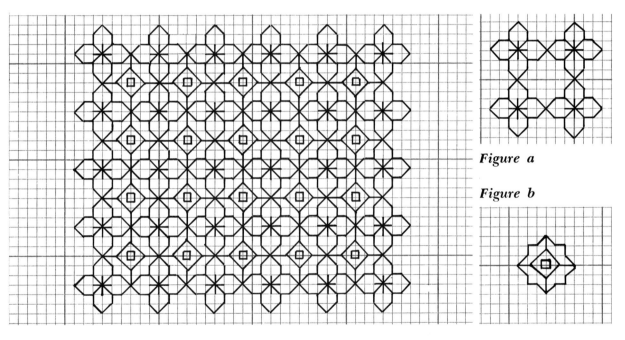

*Figure a*

*Figure b*

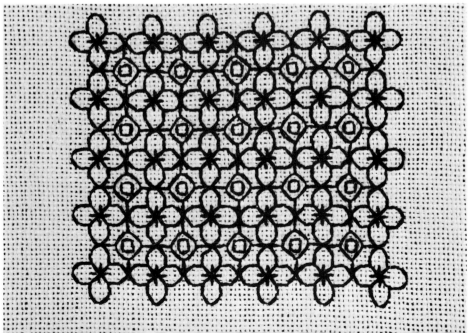

# Pattern No. 16

This large pattern requires careful concentration. First, work the motif in Figure a, then attach the 4 petals to the center Cross stitch. Each unit is 4 threads apart and linked together by a Cross Stitch and a diamond.

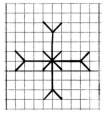

*Figure a*

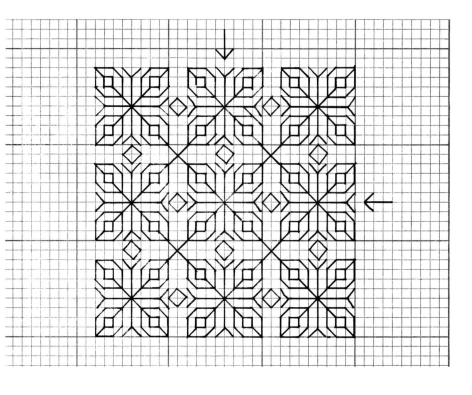

*Figure b*

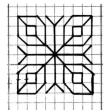

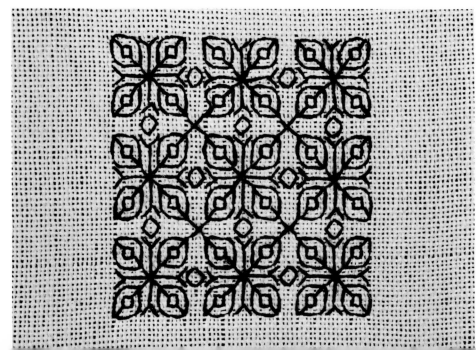

## MEDIUM PATTERNS

# *Pattern No. 17*

This cross motif can be worked very simply over 2 threads using Double Running Stitch or Back Stitch.

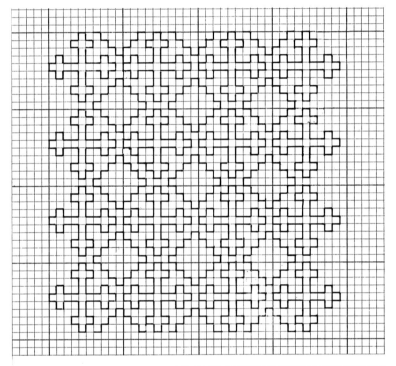

# Pattern No. 18

A perfect pattern for beginners. It is worked over 2 threads in Double Running stitch. The Cross stitches are 2 threads square.

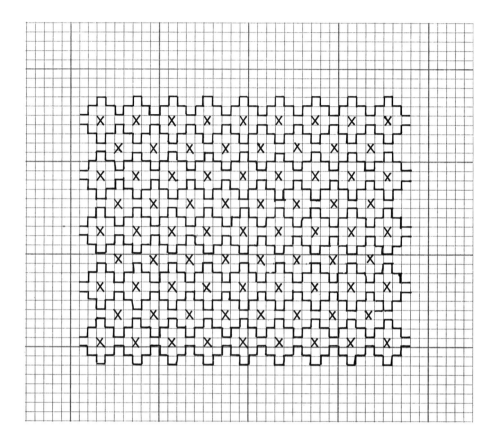

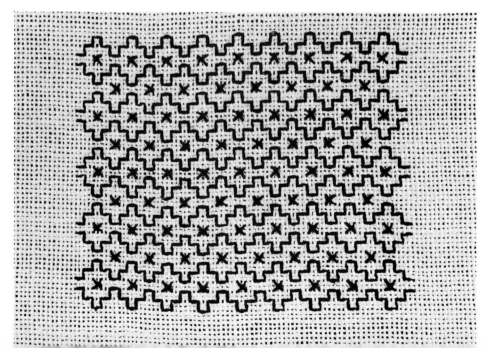

# Pattern No. 19

The Greek-key inspired pattern is worked over 2 threads in Double Running Stitch or Back Stitch. A single row of this pattern makes a lovely border.

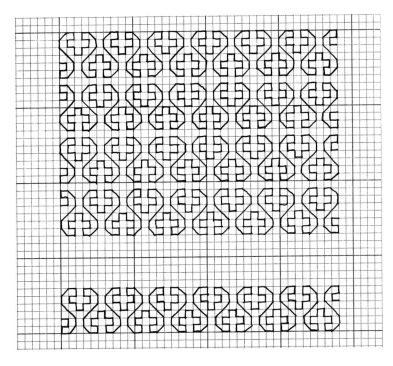

# Pattern No. 20

This is a similar pattern to Pattern #13 but gives a lighter effect because of the areas left unstitched. The whole design is worked in Back Stitch and Cross Stitch over 2 threads. Try working the cross stitches in a different shade from the Back Stitch—for example, dark and light blue; you will love the effect.

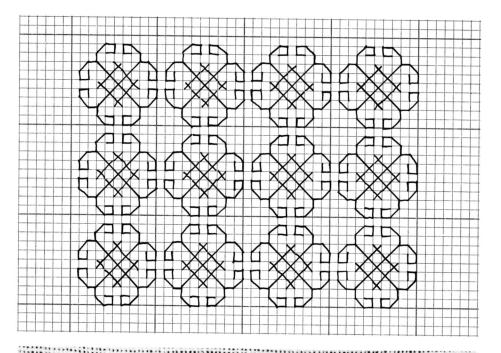

# Pattern No. 21

This pattern is worked over two threads in Back Stitch. The center Cross stitches are worked lastly over 4 threads. A very simple useful pattern.

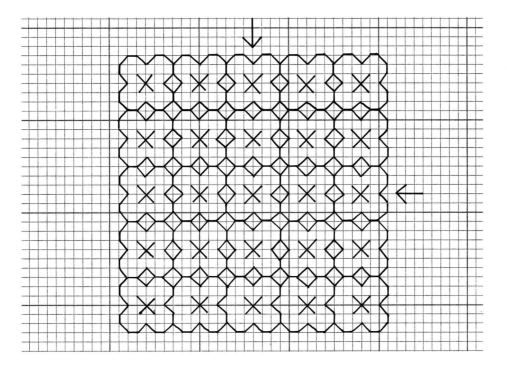

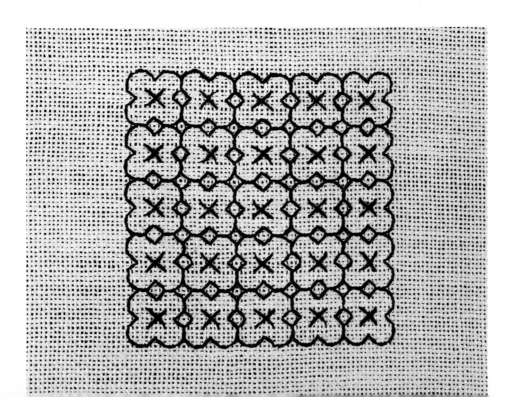

# Pattern No. 22

A dainty pattern resembling flowers. The stitches are worked over 4 threads excepting for the points, which are worked over 2 threads.

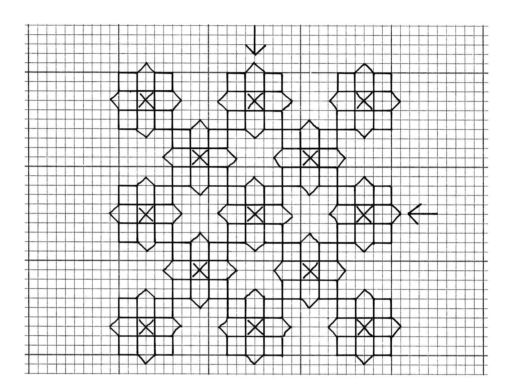

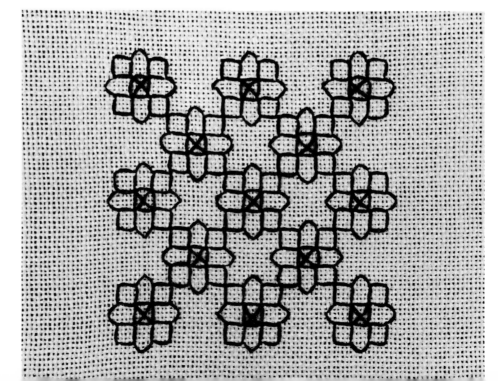

# Pattern No. 23

This is the same motif as in Pattern #22, but because of the arrangement, a darker pattern is achieved.

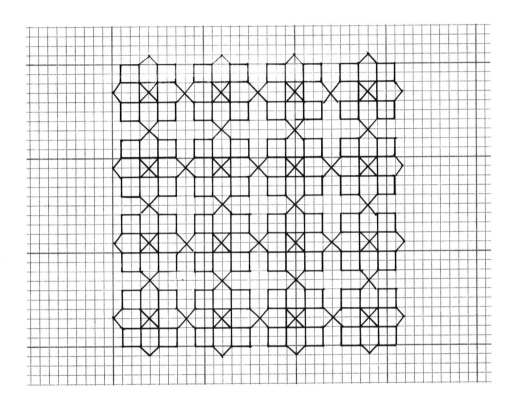

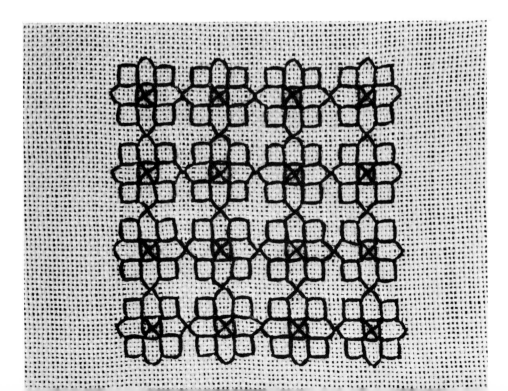

# Pattern No. 24

A feeling of movement is given by this pattern. Each stitch is worked in Back Stitch over 4 threads. This is a very simple fun pattern and one of my favorites. It can be used either horizontally or vertically.

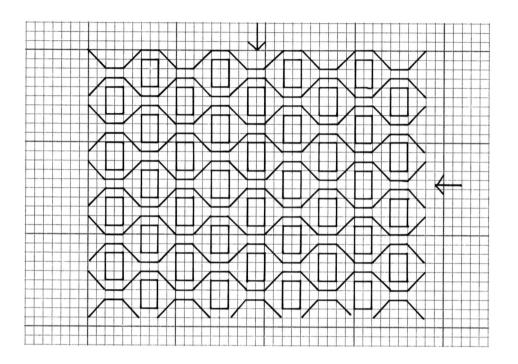

# Pattern No. 25

A lovely pattern with numerous possibilities. The pattern can be easily altered into a heavy pattern or a light pattern by the addition or subtraction of crosses (see sampler on page 107). The boxes should be worked first, then joined together by the diagonal lines. The Cross stitches are then added to the octagonal shapes.

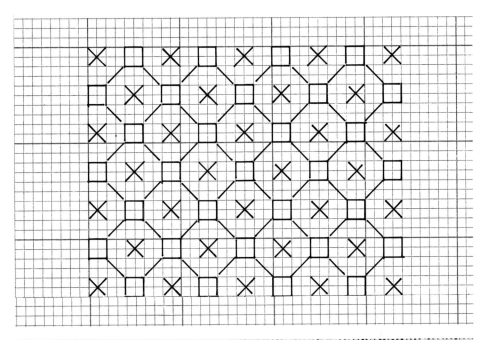

# Pattern No. 26

Another easy pattern worked in Back Stitch over 2 threads.

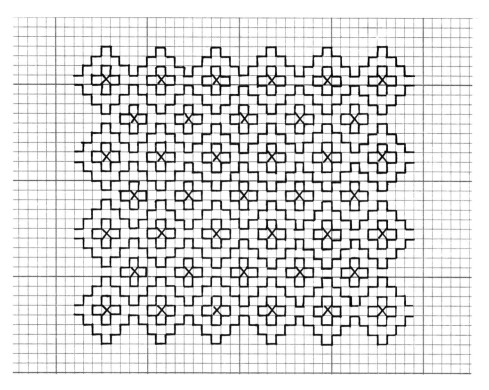

# Pattern No. 27

Try this pattern, using two colors (see tablecloth on Plate 6).
The stitches are worked over 4 threads; a hole appears in the center
of the Eye Stitch.

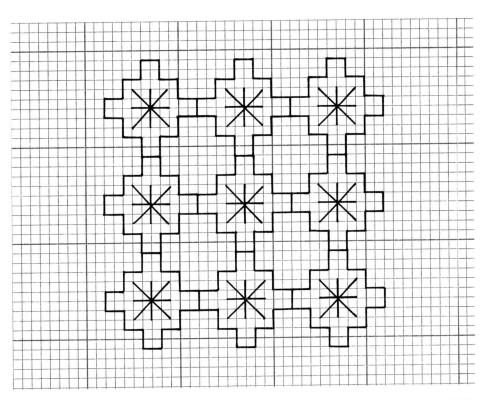

# Pattern No. 28

This pattern also works well in two colors. The basic shape is worked completely in Back or Double Running Stitch over 2 threads. The center Eye Stitch is worked over 2 and 4 threads. This is a lovely pattern that needs a rather large area to be appreciated.

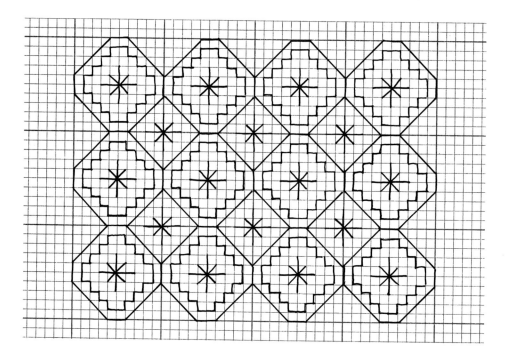

# Pattern No. 29

A medium pattern and one of the simplest to work. This stitch works beautifully in Double Running Stitch, thus making a completely reversible pattern. It can be used either horizontally or vertically.

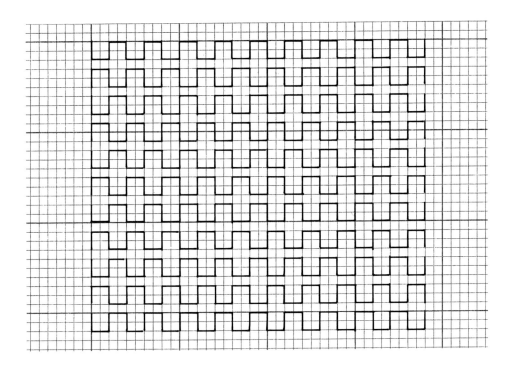

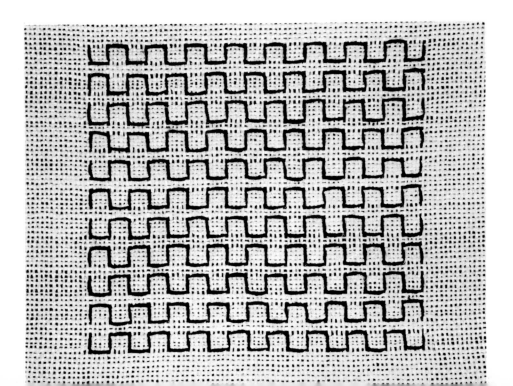

# Pattern No. 30

A Zig-zag Stitch pattern with plenty of movement. The pattern is worked over 2 threads of the fabric and has numerous possibilities, since it can be worked in various directions.

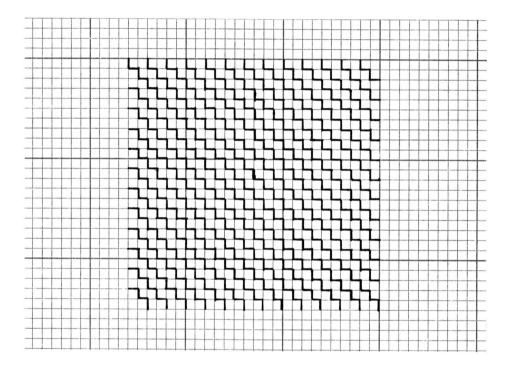

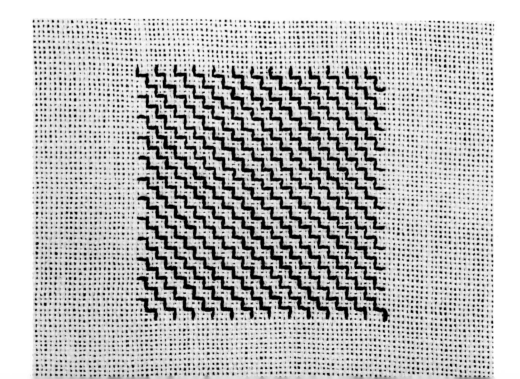

# Pattern No. 31

This is a beatiful pattern and fun to stitch. If worked in the Back Stitch, circles are formed on the wrong side of the fabric.

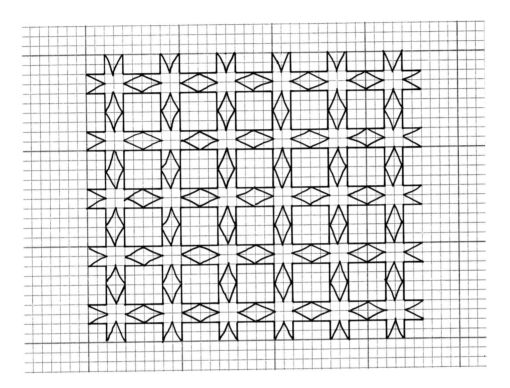

# Pattern No. 32

This circular pattern has a lovely feeling of movement. It is a medium pattern worked in Back Stitch and Eye Stitch. It is a pleasure to stitch.

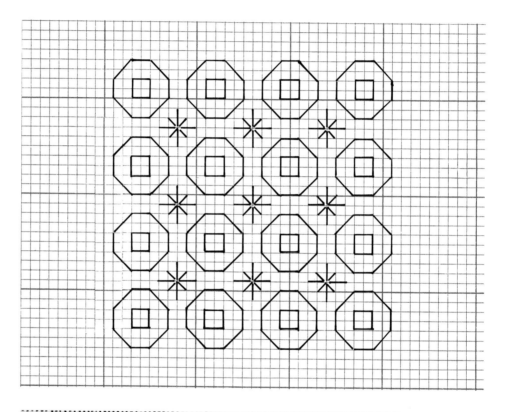

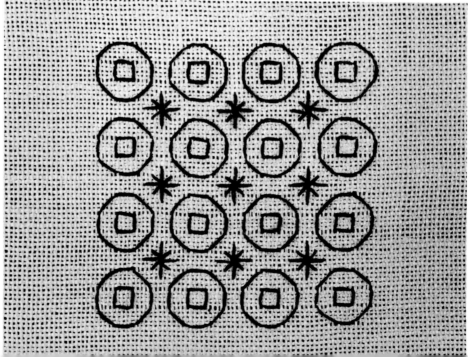

# Pattern No. 33

A very useful, simple pattern worked by alternating a row of Eye stitches with a row of Cross stitches.

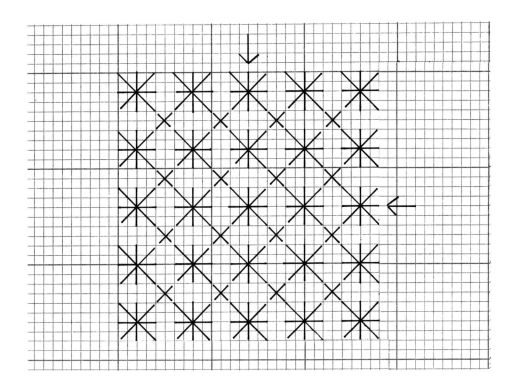

# Pattern No. 34

A medium pattern with a lovely delicate effect. How to work it is clearly shown on page 45.

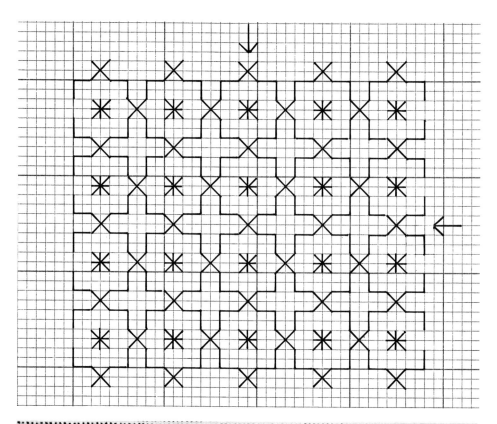

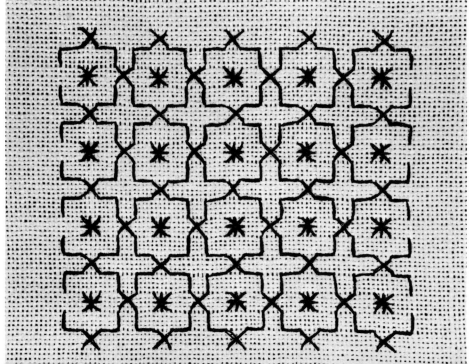

LIGHT PATTERNS

# Pattern No. 35

A pretty effect worked completely in Cross Stitch on the diagonal.

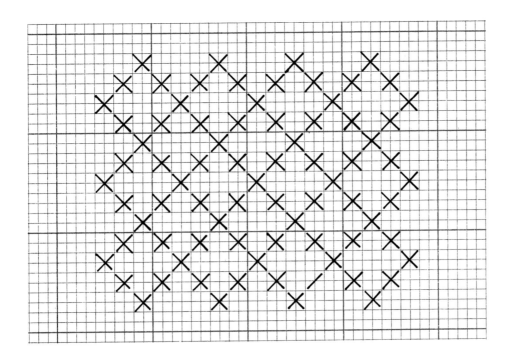

# Pattern No. 36

These pretty flowers are simple to stitch. All the stitches are worked over 4 threads except the Eye Stitch in the center, which is worked over 2 and 4 threads.

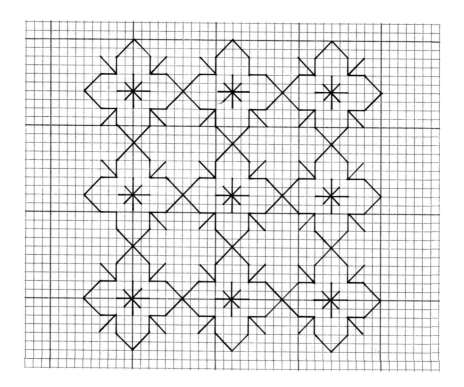

# Pattern No. 37

This is a very delicate pattern worked in Back Stitch over 4 threads.

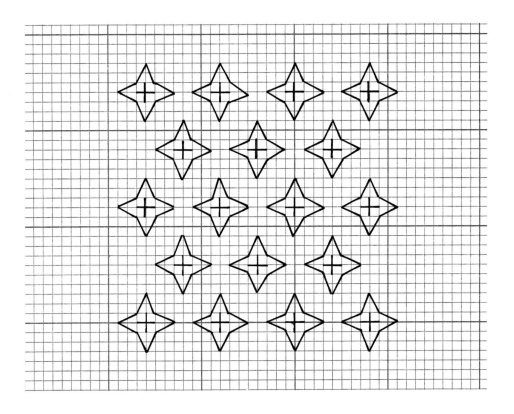

# Pattern No. 38

These vibrant stars are each worked over 4 threads. The pattern produced is very light.

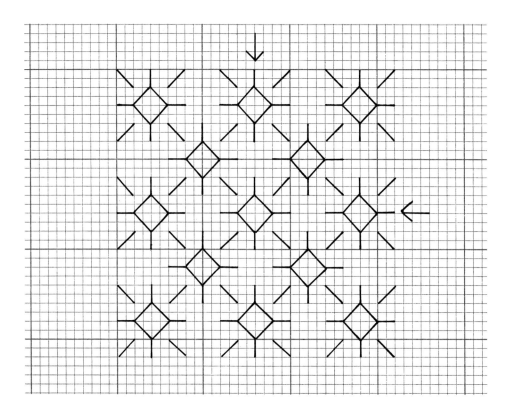

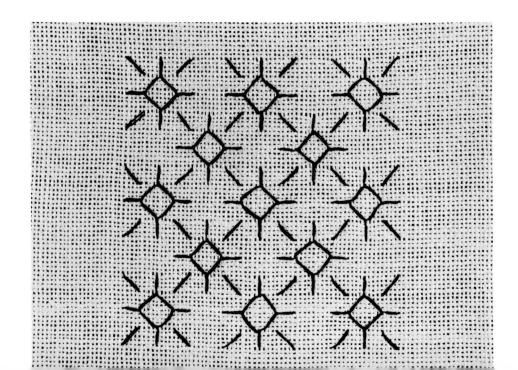

# Pattern No. 39

A lovely pattern worked over 4 threads in Back Stitch and Cross Stitch. A large area is required to show it to its full advantage.

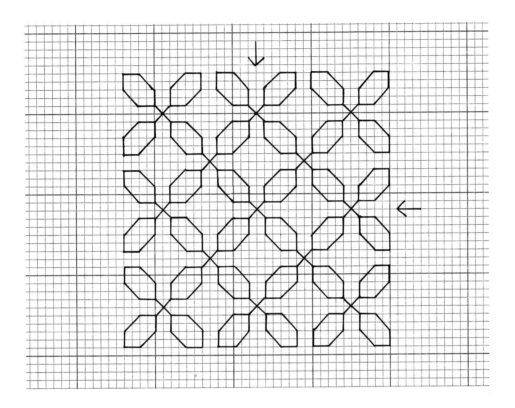

# Pattern No. 40

This pattern is made with a similar motif to that in Pattern #39. A very delicate effect is achieved.

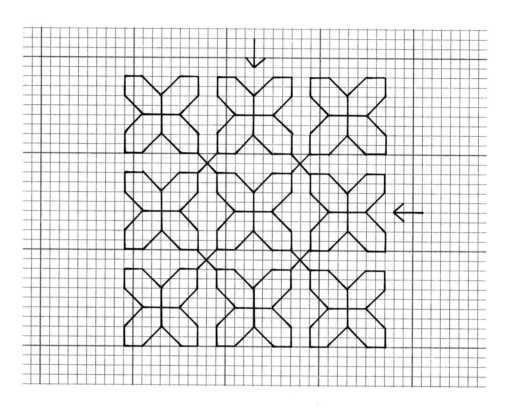

# Pattern No. 41

Begin this pattern with a square and it is simple to stitch.

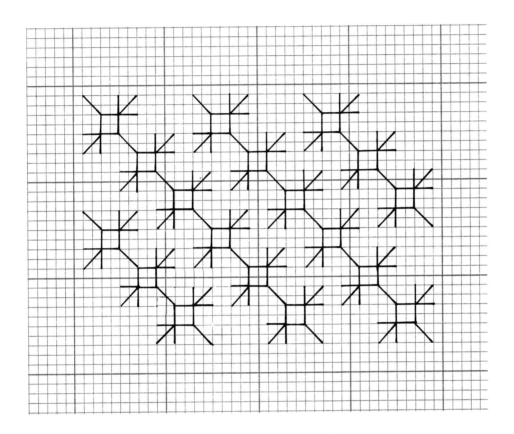

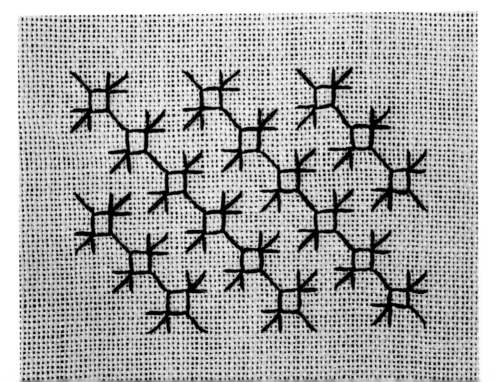

# Pattern No. 42

This is one of the lightest patterns. The pattern is worked over 4 threads in Back and Cross Stitch and can be used either vertically or horizontally.

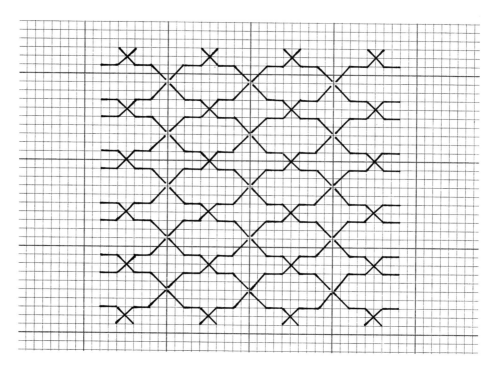

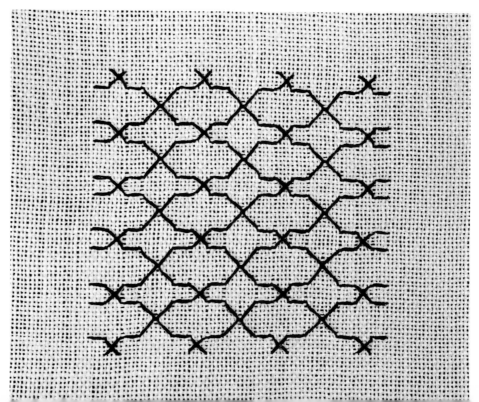

# Pattern No. 43

This pattern gives a very light effect and is a pleasure to stitch. Each Back Stitch is worked over 4 threads.

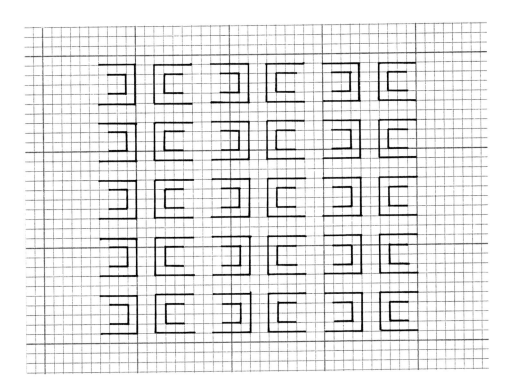

# Pattern No. 44

This is a very large airy pattern. First work an Eye Stitch (Figure a) and then attach a diamond onto each of the 4 straight stitches (Figure b). To the other 4 points of the Eye Stitch attach a diagonal stitch and then a square (Figure c). The next motif is placed 4 threads from the previous one and the squares are joined together.

**Figure a**

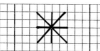

**Figure b**

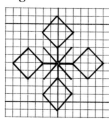

**Figure c**

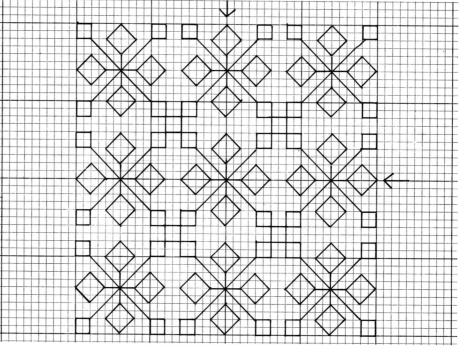

# Pattern No. 45

This large pattern is worked in Cross Stitch and Back Stitch over 4 threads, and because of its simplicity is a pleasure to stitch.

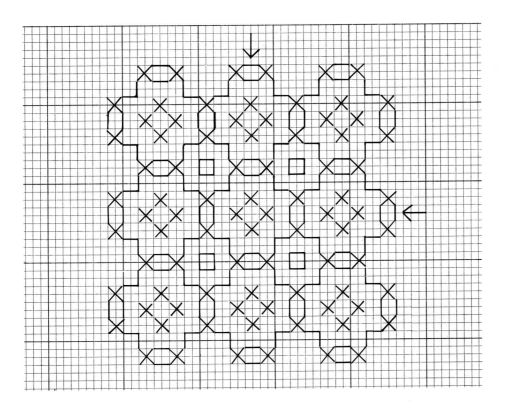

# SOURCES OF
# DESIGN

THE world around us is full of patterns we can adapt to blackwork embroidery. These forms stitched in threads make lovely geometric embroideries.

OPPOSITE:
An iron fence seen in New York City suitable for a blackwork design.

99

Look at the weave of a beautiful basket, draw the pattern it makes on paper, then, on graph paper, make a chart. Now you have created a new blackwork pattern (Figure 20).

Pattern derived from a basket weave.

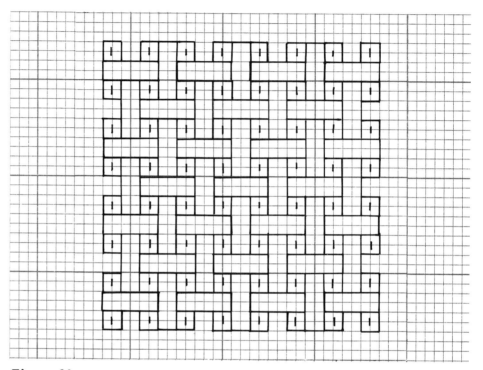

*Figure 20*

A turtle's back makes an interesting blackwork pattern (Figure 21). Local museums hold a wealth of reference material suitable for adaptation to blackwork. Roman and Greek tile designs, mosaics, and

Pattern derived from the design on a turtle's back.

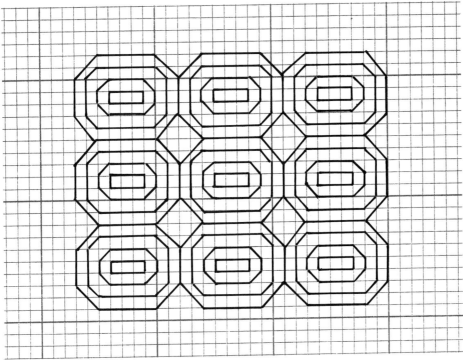

*Figure 21*

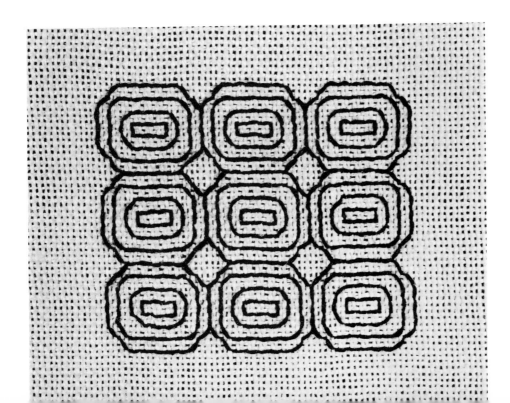

Indian beadwork are all sources for patterns (Figure 22). Ironwork found on gates (Figure 23) or windows (Figure 24) adapts perfectly to blackwork.

Pattern created from a Greek tile.

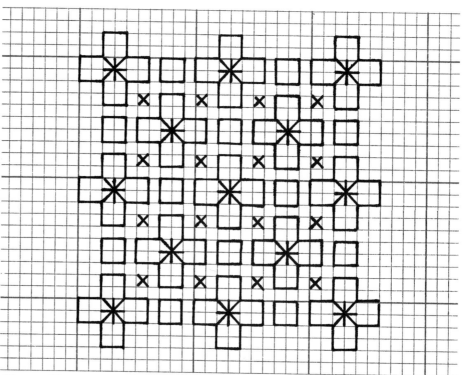

*Figure 22*

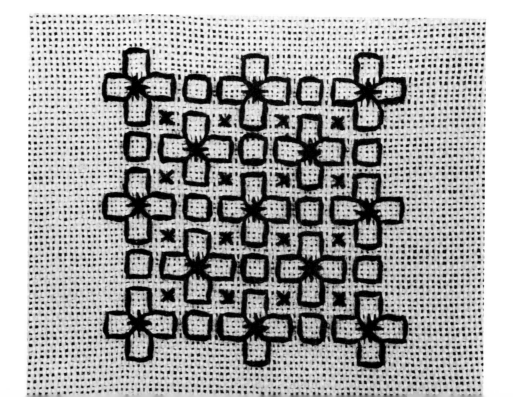

Pattern derived from the iron fence.

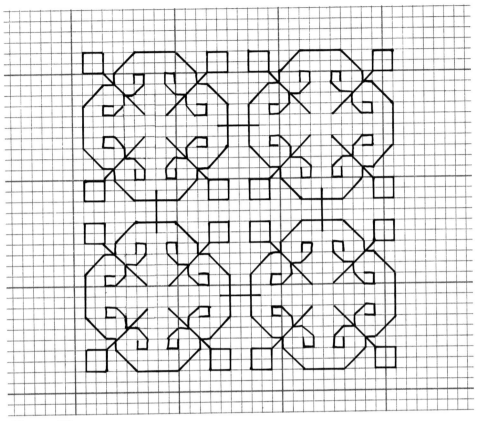

*Figure 23*

Pattern inspired by ironwork covering a window.

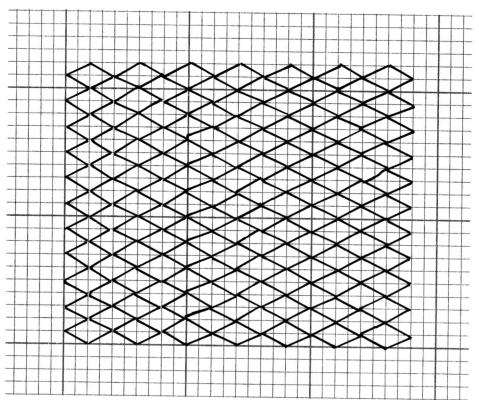

*Figure 24*

Old embroideries can be charted and stitched into patterns. For example, using a magnifying glass, I copied the cuff design from the photograph of Jane Seymour on page 8. I then charted the pattern onto graph paper and embroidered it in Holbein Stitch on linen (Figure 25).

Pattern found on Jane Seymour's cuff.

**Figure 25**

Patterns can also be created by repeating a simple geometric shape such as a square and joining them together in various ways (see graph, Figure 26).

I have worked a sampler showing how simple and effective this technique is. I am sure you can create many more patterns, using diamonds, oblongs, and triangles.

*Figure 26*

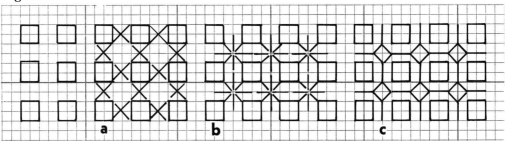

Joining a series of squares with **a.** Cross Stitches, **b.** Eye Stitches, **c.** Diamonds.

Top row, opposite.

New patterns also can be created by adding or omitting parts of existing patterns.

Pattern #25 could be darkened by adding crosses to the squares and changing the Cross stitches to Double Cross Stitch; or lightened by omitting all the Cross stitches (see sampler opposite, second line). Again, on the same sampler, bottom left, Pattern #15 has been changed by adding and omitting motifs. The possibilities are almost endless.

Another way to create new patterns is to change the scale of existing patterns—that is, instead of stitching a pattern over 4 threads of the fabric, work it over 6 threads, thereby producing a lighter effect.

The same results are achieved by using different background fabrics. Fewer threads to the inch enlarge a pattern, more threads reduce it.

Sampler showing various methods of creating new patterns.

The thickness of the yarn used to stitch the patterns also alters the design. The same pattern worked in a thick yarn makes a rich effect, whereas a fine yarn gives a very delicate effect (see Pattern #29 on page 107, bottom right). New patterns can be made also by isolating parts of existing patterns and using them as borders or separate units. Isolated parts also can be embellished to produce more elaborate separate units (see sampler on page 107, center).

Blackwork patterns can also be a source of design for canvas embroidery. I worked the sampler on Plate 2 with tapestry wool and stranded embroidery floss on needlepoint canvas. I first selected Pattern #18 and drew its basic outline shape on graph paper. Three different designs developed from this idea. Then, using a #14 needlepoint canvas—that is, 14 threads to the inch—I stitched the designs in Cross Stitch, Back Stitch, and Eye Stitch over 2 threads of the canvas. The graph shows clearly how to create the patterns, (see graph, Figures 27, 28, and 29). I then chose my favorite design and made a pillow (see Plate 7).

These are some thoughts on how to create your own patterns. I am sure that with all the patterns available you will discover many sources for beautiful blackwork patterns.

**Figure 27**

Step 1.

Work crosses over 2 threads in black tapestry wool using 2 strands.

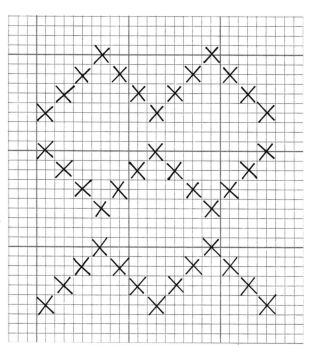

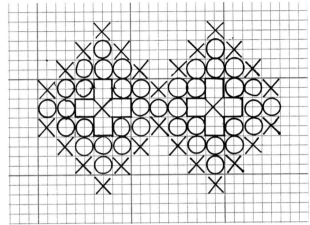

Step 2.

**O** represents cross stitches worked over 2 threads in pale blue tapestry wool.

— Straight stitches are worked in 2 strands of embroidery floss over 2 threads of canvas.

**X** in center is worked in 2 strands of embroidery floss.

*Figure 28*

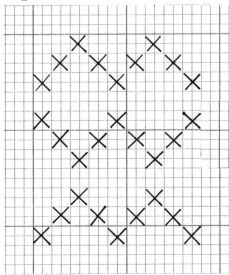

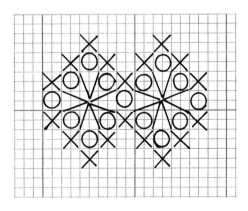

*Figure 29*

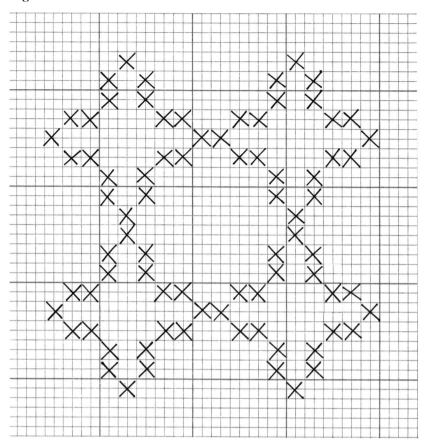

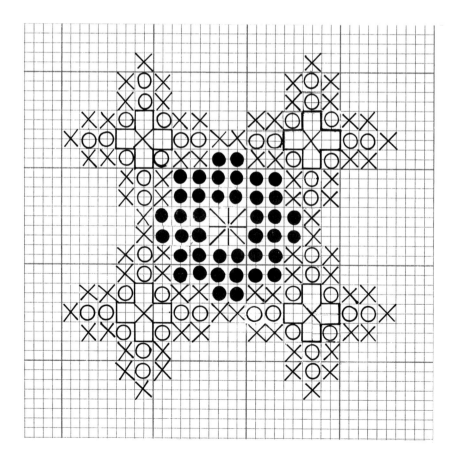

# COLOR IN BLACKWORK

BLACKWORK embroidery was traditionally worked in black with an occasional touch of gold or silver. However, with practice, color can be added to the patterns. If the colors are chosen carefully the delicate balance of light and dark will be retained and a beautiful piece of work will result.

111

Color in blackwork can be used most successfully in two ways. Either by using two contrasting colors such as a green yarn on a blue fabric; or by choosing a main color such as yellow and working with shades of this main color. For added accents a contrasting color could be introduced (see photograph of yellow pillow on Plate 5).

Remember that the striking effect of blackwork is created by the contrast of the black patterns on the white background. So avoid using many different colors, or a busy, confused piece will be the result.

When you are working with gold or silver yarns, use short pieces of yarn, about 12″ or 24″ (doubled if a heavier yarn is needed) in your needle. Gold and silver added as color to the patterns give a very striking and simple effect (see Plate 2).

# BLACKWORK PATTERNS IN FREE-FORM SHAPES

IN the previous chapters all the blackwork patterns have been worked in geometric designs. However, blackwork can be used as a filling for free shapes. Early blackwork pieces were often worked in this way. A shape such as a leaf was outlined and then filled in with various blackwork patterns. The patterns chosen to fill in the shapes produce the light, medium, and dark effects essential for a well-balanced design.

The first step is to draw your design on paper and shade in the areas with dark, medium, and light. The dark areas will be filled with dark patterns, the medium areas with medium patterns, and the light areas with light patterns.

Draw fairly large shapes in some areas of the design so that the patterns can be shown off to their best advantage.

If you don't want to draw your own design, you can trace the line drawing of the mushrooms on page 130.

Now that your design is drawn on paper and the patterns you are going to use are chosen, there are a few new stitches you need to prac-

Woman's coif, white linen embroidered in black silk. English late 16th Century. (*Courtesy of the Victoria and Albert Museum.* Crown copyright)

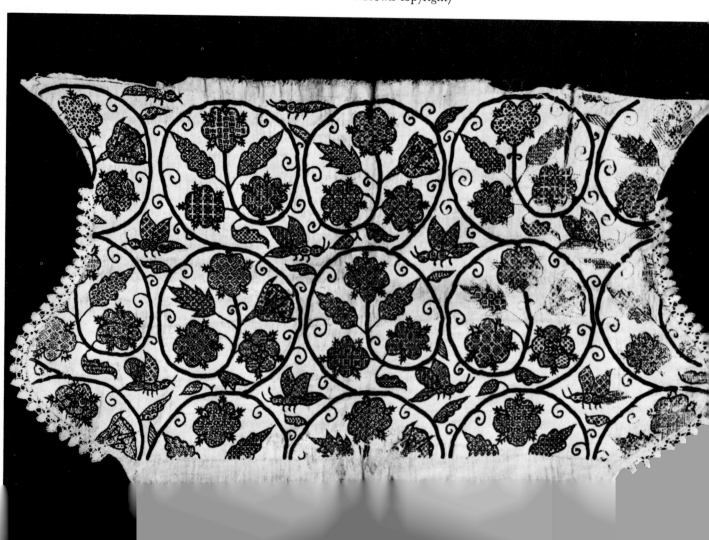

tice. These stitches are Stem Stitch, Chain Stitch, Couching, and Satin Stitch. The working of these stitches is clearly shown in the diagrams. Stem Stitch, Chain Stitch, and Couching are used to outline the shapes before filling in the patterns. Since these stitches are *not* worked in between the fabric threads, a needle with a point called a *crewel* needle is used for the stitchery. A pointed needle is used, because the point must pierce the fabric threads so as to make an accurate outline.

Satin Stitch often is used in conjunction with the blackwork patterns to fill in very small areas, or when gold or silver threads are used. Here again, to produce an accurate shape a pointed needle is used. The next step is to transfer your drawing onto the fabric:

1. Trace your drawing onto heavy tracing paper.

2. Iron the piece of fabric flat.

3. Tape the fabric flat and square onto a hard surface (a drawing board is good).

4. Place the tracing paper on top of the fabric, being sure to place the drawing in the exact position you want it to be reproduced.

5. Hold the tracing paper down firmly; thumb tacks can be placed in all four corners to prevent the tracing paper and fabric from slipping.

6. Very *carefully* slip dressmaker's carbon paper (available at most department stores) in between the tracing paper and fabric. The carbon side of the paper lies toward the fabric. A heavy weight, such as a paperweight, can be placed on top of the tracing paper to hold everything firmly in place, as it is very important that the drawing and fabric do not slip.

7. Using a very hard pencil, trace the outline of the drawing *very heavily* onto the fabric. Check, by lifting up a corner of the tracing paper, to ensure that the drawing is being transferred clearly onto the fabric.

When the complete drawing is traced, remove the tracing paper and carbon paper and you are ready to embroider.

Always begin to stitch the patterns in the center of each shape to achieve the best finished effect. Some people prefer to work the patterns first and then outline the shapes in an outline stitch, whereas others work all the outlines first and then fill in the patterns. Either way is suitable and really depends on the preference of the embroiderer.

# STITCHES FOR FREE-FORM SHAPES

## *STEM STITCH*

Work from left to right and when working around curves work the stitches slightly smaller to give a smoother effect.

Come up at A, in at B, and out at C.

Then go in at D and out again in the same hole made at B. Continue until the row is worked. A continuous line will result. Be sure to keep the thread below the needle when stitching.

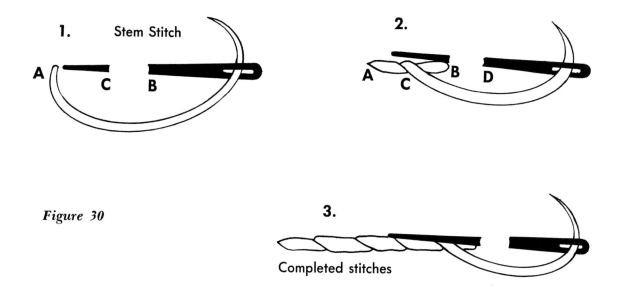

*Figure 30*

## CHAIN STITCH

Come up at A.

Go down again at A and out at B, looping the yarn under the point of the needle.

Repeat, always going back into the same hole where the yarn came out. Small back stitches occur on the wrong side.

*Figure 31*

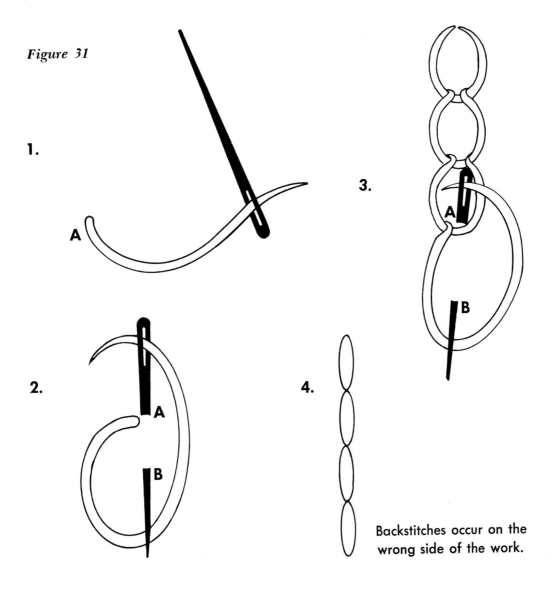

1.

2.

3.

4.

Backstitches occur on the wrong side of the work.

## COUCHING

Couching is a method of holding down one or more threads, often gold threads, with another thread.

Lay the thread to be couched along the line to be outlined. Bring the needle up at A and down at B, over the thread to be couched. Repeat at intervals along the thread.

When the line is complete, take each end of the couched thread onto the wrong side of the work and fasten off the ends.

*Figure 32*

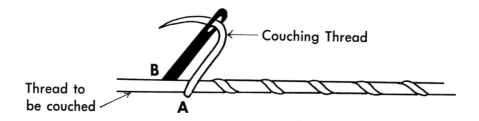

## SATIN STITCH

Satin Stitch produces a solid area and should be used only to fill in small shapes.

Starting at the center of the shape come up at A and go down again at B.

Come up again at C, close to the previous stitch.

Working the straight stitches close together, fill in the shape.

The stitches can also be worked slanted. The slant makes a smoother finished shape.

*Figure 33*

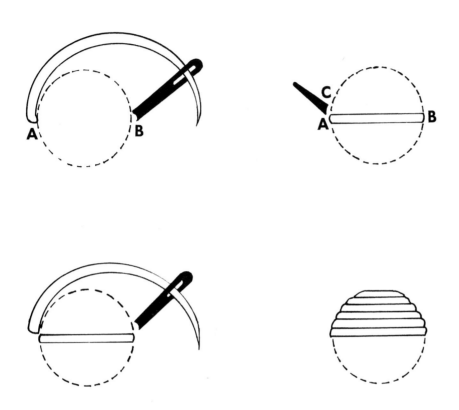

Stitch worked in a
slant across the shape.

# THE DESIGNS

ON the following pages are 24 designs created from the blackwork patterns. These are ideas for you to work with. You can use the designs just as they are, or by changing the colors, fabrics, yarns, or scale of the pattern create your own designs.

If you like the tablecloth idea, but your china is white and gold, change the colors to suit your decor. Or try the butterfly design using only dark patterns to fill in the shapes.

Go ahead and experiment and have fun with the patterns.

OPPOSITE:
Three pillow designs showing the contrasts between a dark, medium and light pattern.

121

# *Eyeglass Case 7¹/₂" x 3"*

SEE COLOR PLATE 3.

## MATERIALS

2 pieces of white even-weave linen, 9½" x 5½" (22 threads per inch)

2 pieces of felt for the lining, 9½" x 5½"

1 skein of dark blue stranded embroidery floss

1 skein medium blue stranded embroidery floss

1 skein of light blue embroidery floss

#22 tapestry needle

## INSTRUCTIONS

1. Follow step 2 for "Starting a Project" on page 39.

2. Fold one piece of linen in half lengthwise and baste a line down the fold. (This is the position for the dark blue center point of the pattern.)

3. On your sampler practice the pattern darning (see photograph on page 24) and the color sequence used—for example:

8 rows of dark blue  
8 rows of medium blue ⎫  
8 rows of light blue ⎬ twice  
8 rows of dark blue ⎭

Use 3 strands of embroidery floss and work each stitch over 4 threads and under 4 threads and one thread apart.

4. Fill the piece of linen with the pattern darning, working the dark blue center point of the pattern down the basting line (see photograph on page 41).

5. To complete:

    a. Place the embroidered piece and the linen right sides together and stitch around the two long sides and across one short side.

    b. Turn the case onto the right side and square out the corners.

    c. Make the lining in the same manner as the case but do not turn it right side out.

    d. Insert the lining into the case.

    e. Turn the top raw edge of the lining and of the case onto the wrong side and slip-stitch the lining to the case.

# *Book Jacket*

## MATERIALS

A hard-back book to be covered
Black embroidery floss
A piece of even-weave linen, 2″ larger all around than the opened book
#22 tapestry needle

## INSTRUCTIONS

1. Measure the front, spine, and back of the book. With a basting stitch outline these areas on the linen, basting a center line down the spine. Leave an extra 2″ of fabric all around (Figure 34a).

2. Turn a single ½″ hem all around the linen and hand- or machine-stitch.

3. On your sampler, practice Pattern #8, using 2 strands of embroidery floss.

4. Fill the front cover area of the book with Pattern #8. On the spine area work single motifs down the center line. Each motif is 6 threads apart.

5. If you wish, embroider the back of the book.

6. To make up the book cover:
    a. Press the finished embroidery (see page 47).
    b. Turn back the front and back flaps to the basting line and stitch (Figure 34b).
    c. Turn the embroidery onto the right side, squaring out the corners.
    d. Slip the book into the pockets.

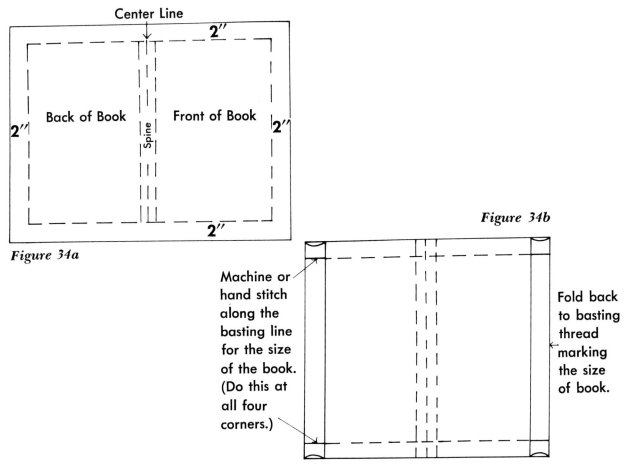

Center Line

2″

Back of Book          Front of Book

2″          Spine          2″

2″

*Figure 34a*

*Figure 34b*

Machine or hand stitch along the basting line for the size of the book. (Do this at all four corners.)

Fold back to basting thread marking the size of book.

Embroidered book jacket.

# *Sampler Bag* *approximately 14" x 14"*

A selection of patterns were stitched on a sampler and then made into a workbag (see photograph on page 36).

## MATERIALS

1 finished piece of embroidery, 15" x 15"
1 piece of even-weave linen, 15" x 15"
2 pieces of cotton (I chose blue), 15" x 15"
1 pair of wooden handles

## INSTRUCTIONS

1. Baste the embroidered piece and the linen right sides together. Machine- or hand-stitch along the bottom and 11" up on either side. Leave the top completely open.
2. Turn the bag onto the right side, press the seams.
3. Make the lining in the same manner as the bag.
4. Do not turn the lining right side out.
5. Insert it into the bag.
6. Turn the raw edges of the sides of the bag and the lining to the wrong side and slip-stitch the lining to the bag.
7. Insert the tops of the bag into the slots of the wooden handles, turn over about 1", and slip-stitch to the lining.

# Leaf Pillow  *14" x 14"*

## MATERIALS

2 pieces of even-weave linen, 16" x 16" (22 threads per inch),
  or 2 white linen table napkins
3 skeins of black embroidery floss
colored basting thread
Pillow form, 14" x 14"
#22 tapestry needle

## INSTRUCTIONS

1. Follow steps 1 and 2 of "Starting a Project" on page 39.

2. Fold one piece of fabric in half lengthwise and down this fold work a row of back stitches over 2 threads, using 2 strands of embroidery floss.

3. Fold the fabric in half widthwise and, starting from the center, work a row of back stitches over 2 threads along this fold. Start from the center so that the back stitches in the center are worked in the same hole. Count 4 threads away from the row of back stitches and work a row of running stitches, over 2 threads and under 2 threads (see Figure 35 for position of rows of stitching).

5. The piece is now divided into 4 squares. Finally, baste a square 7″ from either side and top and bottom of the center point. This marks the stitching line for the finished pillow.

6. Trace the leaf shape below onto a piece of tracing paper (Figure 36).

7. Following the instructions on page 115, transfer the leaf shape onto each square, placing each leaf as shown in the photograph.

8. On your sampler, practice Pattern #6 and stem-stitch. Using two strands of embroidery floss, stem-stitch around the outline of each leaf shape. Finally, fill each leaf with Pattern #6.

9. To make up the pillow: Follow the instructions beginning at step 9 on page 47, omitting the eyelet ribbon.

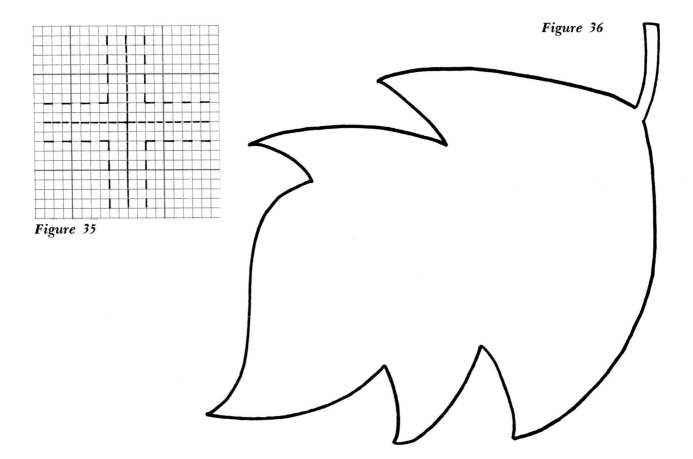

*Figure 36*

*Figure 35*

Butterfly picture.

The gold butterfly adds a striking yet simple touch to this design.

PLATE 1

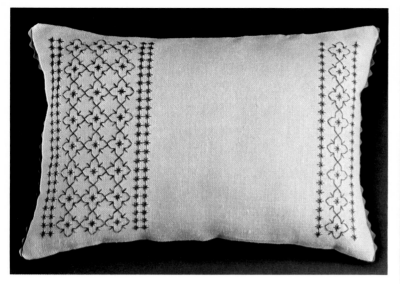

A contrasting effect is achieved by working green embroidery on blue linen.

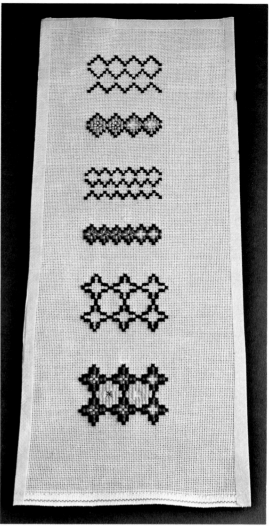

Canvas sampler.

Blackwork patterns enhanced with gold threads.

PLATE 2

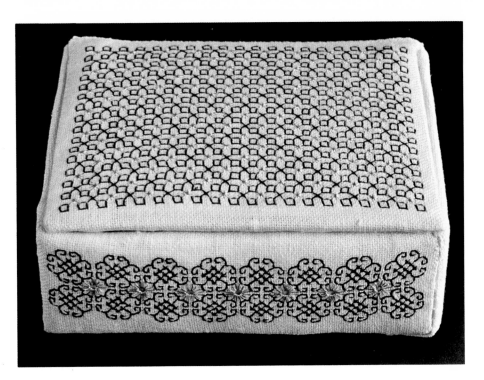

Embroidered box.

Eye glass case.

Place mat and napkin.

PLATE 3

Brown and blue pillow.

Beige and white pillow.

PLATE 4

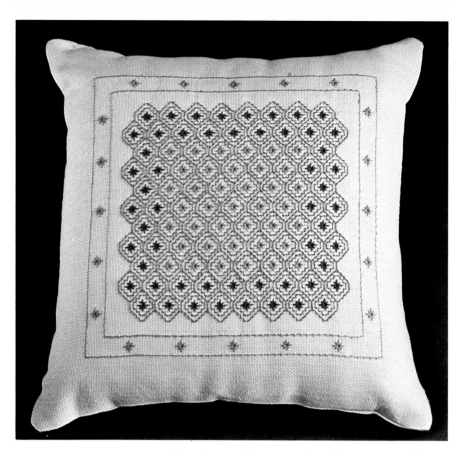

Yellow linen pillow embroidered in orange and brown
with green used as a contrasting color.

Pink pillow.

PLATE 5

Completed table cloth.

Close-up showing color arrangement for the table cloth design.

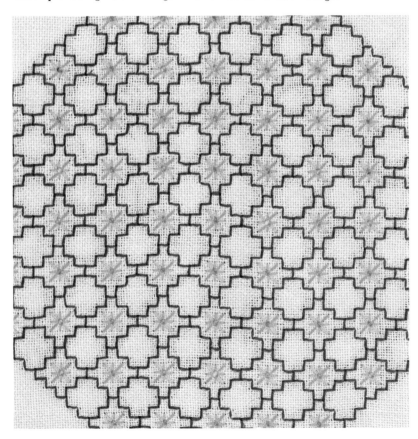

PLATE 6

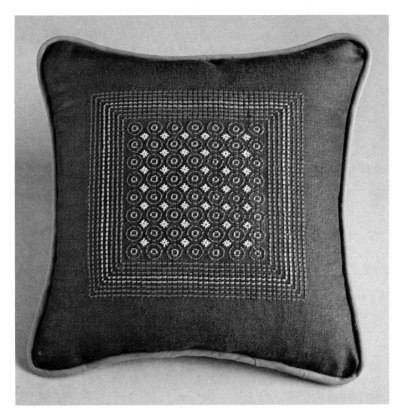

Red and orange pillow.

Pillow worked in canvas embroidery is inspired by pattern #18.

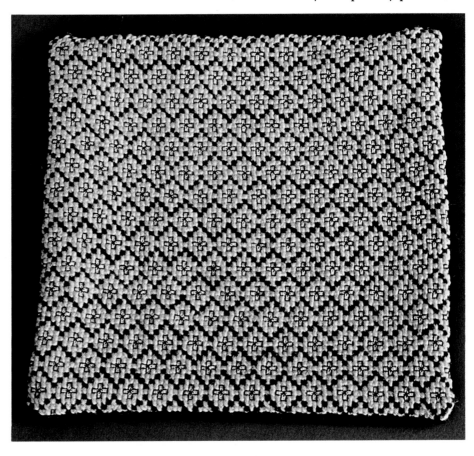

PLATE 7

The yoke of a child's dress decorated with blackwork embroidery.

Embroidery worked in brown on a beige cotton blouse.

PLATE 8

# Three Mushrooms
## *11" x 8" (Inside Frame)*

## MATERIALS

1 piece of even-weave linen, 10" x 13" (22 threads per inch)
3 skeins of black embroidery floss
#22 tapestry needle

## INSTRUCTIONS

1. Begin with step 2 of "Starting a Project," on page 39.

2. Trace the mushroom design on page 130 onto a piece of tracing paper (Figure 37).

3. Follow the instructions on page 115 and transfer the design onto the linen.

4. On your sampler, practice the Stem Stitch and Patterns #1, 2, 15, 18, 26, 29, and 30, using 3 strands of embroidery floss.

5. Outline all the shapes in Stem Stitch and then fill in the patterns as indicated by the numbers on the drawing.

6. Press the piece flat and frame as a picture or sew into a pillow.

*Figure 37*

# Lace Pillow *14″ x 14″*

## MATERIALS

2 pieces of white even-weave linen, 16″ x 16″ (22 threads per inch), or 2 white linen table napkins

1 skein of black embroidery floss

1 ¾ yds. of 2″ white eyelet ribbon

Colored basting thread

Pillow form, 14″ x 14″

#22 tapestry needle

## INSTRUCTIONS

1. Follow steps 1, 2, and 3A of "Starting a Project," on page 39.

2. Marking the design area and marking the border area are clearly explained on the graph below (Figure 38).

**3b.**

*Figure 38*

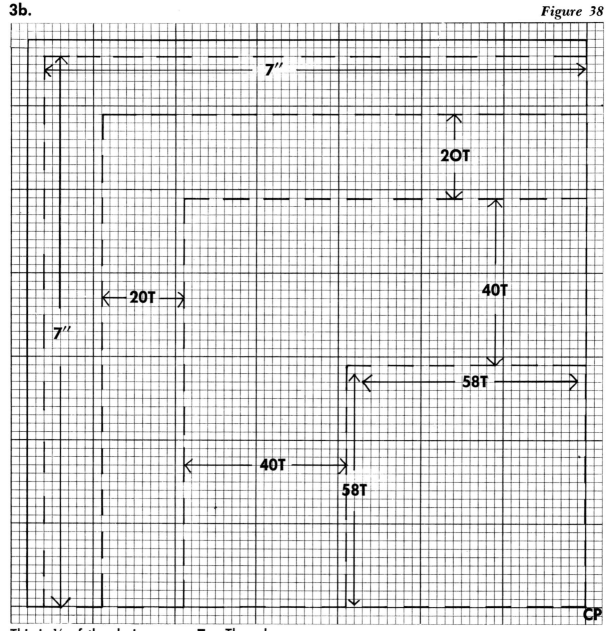

This is ¼ of the design.        **T** = Threads

**CP** = Center Point        Each small square = 2 threads.

3. On the sampler, practice Pattern #39, using 2 strands of the embroidery floss. All the stitches are worked over 4 threads of the fabric.

4. Begin at the center point of Pattern #39 and work a cross stitch. This will be the exact center of your pillow. (The basting lines marking the center will run in the middle of the Cross Stitch.) Now work 25 motifs of the pattern. They will fit into the square marked by the basting threads. Next, work 8 single motifs around the border area of the pillow (see basting lines), arranging them one on each of the center lines and one squarely in each corner. (They will be each 88 threads apart.) Refer to the photograph of the pillow on page 131 to check the design arrangement.

5. To make up the pillow: Follow the instructions beginning at step 9 on page 47.

# Dark Flowers Pillow *14" x 14"*

## MATERIALS

2 pieces of white even-weave linen, 16" x 16" (22 threads per inch) , or 2 white linen table napkins

Approximately 20 skeins of black embroidery floss

Colored basting thread

Pillow form, 14" x 14"

#22 tapestry needle.

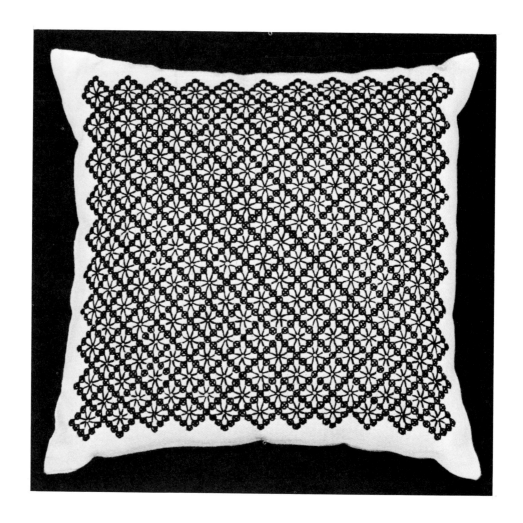

# INSTRUCTIONS

1. Follow steps 1, 2, and 3A of "Starting a Project" on page 39.

2. Baste a square 7″ from either side and top and bottom of the center point. This marks the stitching line for the finished pillow. On your sampler, practice Pattern #14, using 4 strands of embroidery floss. All the stitches are worked over 4 threads of the fabric.

3. Begin at the center point and work a Cross Stitch in the center of your fabric (the basting lines marking the center will run in the middle of the Cross Stitch).

4. Work all the Cross Stitch framework of the pattern, first diagonally across the center of the pillow. There will be 61 crosses in all. Next complete the pattern.

5. To make up the pillow: Follow the instructions beginning at step 9 on page 47, omitting the eyelet ribbon.

# Pink Pillow 14" x 14"

SEE COLOR PLATE 5.

## MATERIALS

> 1 piece of pink even-weave linen, 16" x 16" (22 threads per inch)
> 1 piece of brick-red fabric for pillow backing, 16" x 16"
> 60" of brick-red piping cord
> 1 pillow form, 14" x 14"
> 1 skein of brown embroidery floss (Coats and Clark 51-C)
> 1 skein of brick-red embroidery floss (Coats and Clark #75-A)
> #22 tapestry needle

## INSTRUCTIONS

1. Follow steps 1, 2, and 3A for "Starting a Project" on page 39.

2. Baste a 7" square from either side and top and bottom of the center point. This marks the stitching line for the finished pillow.

3. On your sampler practice Pattern #44, working the flower motif in brick-red and the boxes in brown. Use 3 strands of the embroidery floss.

4. The chart (Figure 39) shows ¼ of the design. The center basting threads go through the center of the Eye stitches. Follow the chart to work the complete design.

5. To make up the pillow: Follow step 9 on page 47, substituting the piping cord for the lace edge.

*Figure 39*

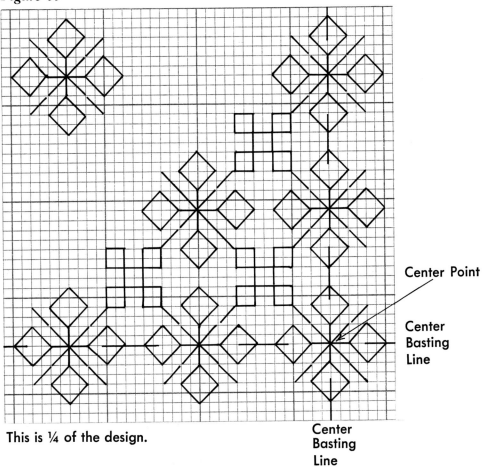

This is ¼ of the design.

Center Point

Center
Basting
Line

Center
Basting
Line

# Brown and Blue Pillow
## *14" x 14"*    SEE COLOR PLATE 4.

## MATERIALS

2 pieces of light-brown even-weave linen (22 threads per inch),
    or 2 even-weave linen table napkins
60" of gold braid
1 pillow form, 14" x 14"
6 skeins of navy-blue embroidery floss (Coats & Clark #55)
10 skeins of brown embroidery floss (Coats & Clark #51-C)
#22 tapestry needle

## INSTRUCTIONS

1. Follow steps 1, 2, and 3A for "Starting a Project" on page 39.

2. Baste a 7" square from either side and top and bottom of the center point. This marks the stitching line for the finished pillow.

3. On your sampler practice Pattern #13, the Cross Stitch, and one row of Pattern #29. This is for the border. Work Pattern #13 over 4 threads instead of 2, and work all the Cross stitches on the pillow in navy-blue floss. Use 6 strands of embroidery floss throughout.

4. The center box of Pattern #13 is worked over the center point of the pillow (see graph in Figure 40) and 9 motifs in all are worked. The border is worked 4 threads away from the design. For working the border, follow the graph (Figure 40).

5. To make up the pillow: Follow step 9 on page 47, omitting the lace. When the pillow is completed, hand-sew the gold braid around the 4 sides.

*Figure 40*

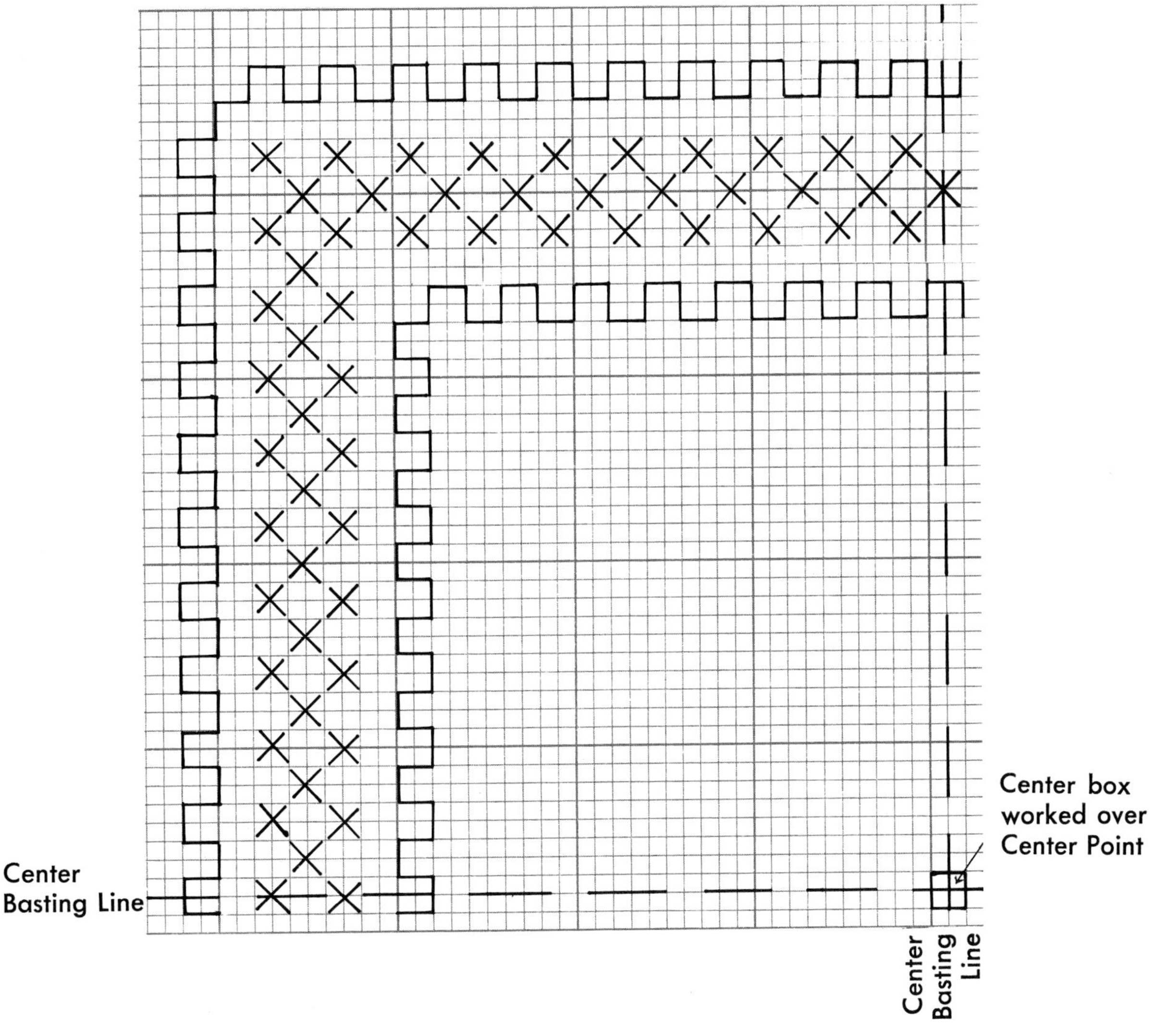

Center Basting Line

Center Basting Line

Center box worked over Center Point

# Orange and Yellow Pillow
## 14" x 14"    SEE COLOR PLATE 5.

## MATERIALS

2 pieces of even-weave yellow linen 16" x 16", (22 threads per inch)

2 skeins of orange embroidery floss

2 skeins of brown embroidery floss

2 skeins of green embroidery floss

Colored basting thread

Pillow form, 14" x 14"

#22 tapestry needle

## INSTRUCTIONS

1. Follow steps 1, 2, and 3A of "Starting a Project" on page 39.

2. Next, count from the center point 72 threads to the left and 72 threads to the right, stitch a basting thread down either side. Then count 70 threads above the center point and 70 threads below. Stitch a basting thread above and below.

3. Count 8 threads to each side of the design area and baste another square. Then count 12 threads from this line and baste a second square. Finally baste a square 7" from either side and top and bottom of the center point. This makes the stitching area of the finished pillow.

4. On your sampler, practice the Double Running Stitch and Pattern #28, working it in the appropriate colors and using 3 strands of the embroidery floss.

5. Using orange floss, stitch the center Eye Stitch as shown on the graph (Figure 41a). Then stitch all the green Back Stitch framework

(you will make 93 diamond shapes in all). Finally, stitch the remaining 92 Eye stitches. Copy the color arrangement from the color photograph on Plate 5 (there are 54 brown Eye Stitches). The orange border is worked in Double Running Stitch over 2 threads. The Eye stitches inside the border are 24 threads apart (see chart for center Eye Stitch of border, Figure 41b). Work the center Eye stitches on each of the four sides and the corners will follow perfectly.

6. To make up the pillow: Follow the instructions beginning at step 9 on page 47, omitting the eyelet ribbon.

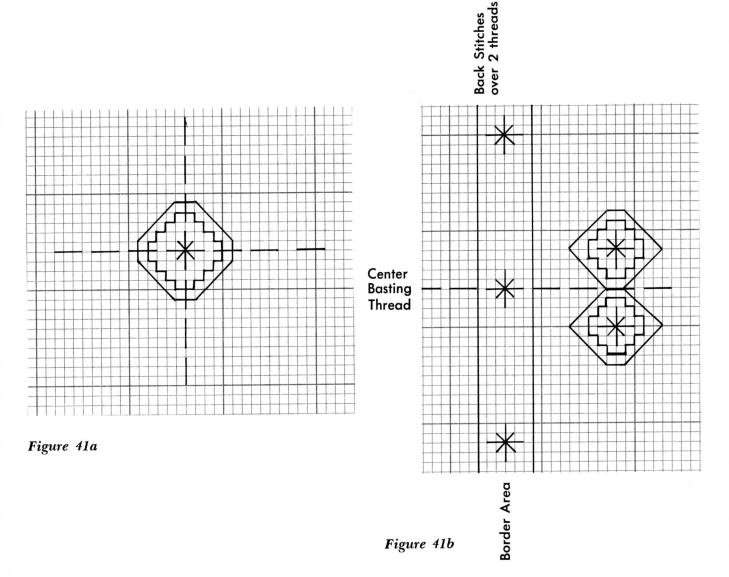

*Figure 41a*

Back Stitches over 2 threads

Center Basting Thread

Border Area

*Figure 41b*

# Beige and White Pillow
## 14" x 14"

SEE COLOR PLATE 4.

## MATERIALS

2 pieces of even-weave linen, 16" x 16" (22 threads per inch),
 or 2 white linen table napkins
2 skeins of beige embroidery floss (Coats and Clark #214)
Colored basting thread
Pillow form, 14" x 14"
#22 tapestry needle

## INSTRUCTIONS

1. Follow steps 1, 2, and 3A of "Starting a Project" on page 39.

2. Count 62 threads from either side and top and bottom of the center point and stitch a basting line forming a square. From this square, count 44 threads from either side and top and bottom and baste a second square.

Baste a square 7" from either side and top and bottom of the center point. This marks the stitching area for the pillow.

3. On your sampler practice the Back Stitch and Pattern #31, using 2 strands of the embroidery floss.

4. Work the pattern inside the two basting lines as shown on the graph Figure 42). Then work a row of Back stitches (4 threads away from the pattern) to form the 2 squares marked by the basting

threads. The center line runs through the middle of the center Back
Stitch.

5. To make up the pillow: Follow the instructions beginning
at step 9 on page 47.

*Figure 42*

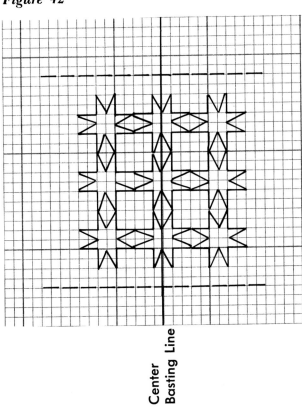

Center
Basting Line

# *Red and Orange Pillow*
## *12" x 12"*

SEE COLOR PLATE 7.

## MATERIALS

    1 piece of red even-weave linen, 14" x 14" (28 threads per inch)
    1 piece of orange fabric for pillow backing, 14" x 14"
    50" of orange piping cord
    1 pillow form, 12" x 12"
    #22 tapestry needle
    1 skein of beige embroidery floss (DMC #842)
    1 skein of dark orange embroidery floss (DMC #608)
    1 skein of light orange embroidery floss (DMC #970)

## INSTRUCTIONS

    1. Follow steps 1, 2, and 3A for "Starting a Project" on page 39. NOTE: for step 1, cut linen 14" x 14".

Baste a square 6" from either side and top and bottom of the center point. This marks the stitching line for the finished pillow.

    2. On your sampler, practice the Back Stitch, using 6 strands of the embroidery floss, and Pattern #32, using 3 strands of the floss. The circles are worked in dark orange, the boxes in light orange, and the Eye Stitch in beige. The color sequence for the Back Stitch is 3 rows dark orange, 3 rows light orange, then 3 rows dark orange (check color photo on Plate 7).

    3. The chart (Figure 43) gives ¼ of the design. Position the

motifs on the center lines as shown and work the complete design. The Back stitches are worked over 4 threads.

4. To make up the pillow: Follow step 9 on page 47, substituting the piping cord for the lace edge.

NOTE: As I wanted a delicate effect, I made the pillow on fine linen. If you use 22 threads per inch, cut a larger piece of linen and backing, and the finished result will be a larger pillow.

*Figure 43*

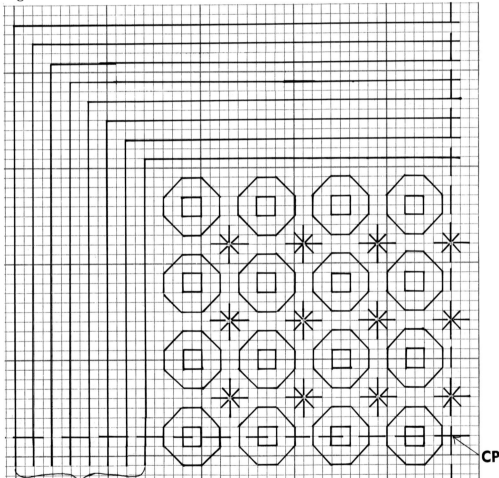

Rows of backstitches
worked over 4 threads.
This is ¼ of the design.

CP = Center Point

# *Blue Linen Pillow* *12" x 18"*

SEE COLOR PLATE 2.

## MATERIALS

1 piece of blue even-weave linen, 20" x 14" (22 threads per inch)
2 skeins of embroidery floss (Coats and Clark #28-B)
1 piece of emerald-green fabric for pillow back, 20" x 14"
26" of emerald-green rickrack braid (13" each piece)
Pillow form, 12" x 18"
#22 tapestry needle

## INSTRUCTIONS

1. Follow steps 1 and 2 for "Starting a Project" on page 39. NOTE: in step 1, cut linen and fabric 20" x 14".

2. On the linen, baste a rectangle 12" x 18" and mark the center threads lengthwise and widthwise with a colored basting thread.

3. On your sampler, practice Patterns #3 and 36, using 3 strands of the embroidery floss. Place the design on the lengthwise basting thread as shown in the graph (Figure 44). Work 8 flowers down each row, 3 rows on the left-hand side of the pillow and 1 row on the right-hand side.

Work 24 Eye stitches down each row, 2 rows on either side of the 3 rows of flowers and 1 row on either side of the single row of flowers. The borders are placed from the center point as follows:

   a. Left-hand border 50 threads
   b. Right-hand border 106 threads

When all the embroidery is finished an area of about 1″ remains around the design.

5. To make up the pillow:

a. Press the embroidery flat.

b. Baste a piece of rickrack braid down both of the 12″ sides. The basting lines match those stitched to mark the rectangle, and are worked down the center of the braid.

c. Next baste the embroidered piece and the green fabric for the pillow back right sides together.

d. Stitch around 3 sides and 1″ in on either side of the fourth side.

e. Turn the pillow to the right side, squaring out the corners and braid.

f. Insert the pillow form and slip-stitch the fourth side closed.

**Figure 44**

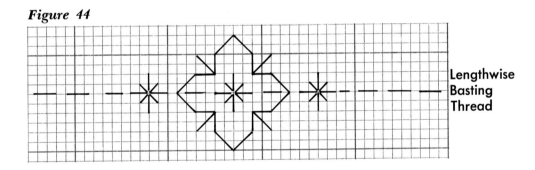

Lengthwise
Basting
Thread

# Place Mat and Napkin
## Place Mat, 17" x 14"; Napkin, 15" x 15"

SEE COLOR PLATE 3.

## MATERIALS

2 pieces of blue even-weave linen (1 piece for place mat, 20" x 17", 1 piece for napkin, 18" x 18")

3 skeins of purple embroidery floss

#22 tapestry needle

## INSTRUCTIONS FOR NAPKIN

1. Follow steps 2 and 3a of "Starting a Project" on page 39.

2. At a center basting line, measure 1½" in from any side edge. Then on one side of the center basting line, work a Cross Stitch over 4 threads.

Continue working a row of Cross stitches down the side of the napkin until 34 stitches have been worked. Go back to the center and complete the row (68 cross stitches in all).

Work 68 Cross stitches down each of the other three sides. (A square is made.)

3. In any corner, work one motif of Pattern #16. The center Cross Stitch of the motif is 12 threads away from the border.

4. Turn under and stitch a ¾" hem 14 threads away from the row of Cross stitches.

5. Press the napkin.

# INSTRUCTIONS FOR THE PLACE MAT

1. Repeat steps 1 and 2 for making the napkin, except work the first Cross Stitch on the longest side of the place mat.

2. Continue working a row of Cross stitches down the long side of the mat until 39 stitches are worked. Go back to the center and complete the row (78 crosses in all).

3. Work 59 Cross stitches down the short side, 78 across the long side and 59 down the other short side. (A rectangle is made.)

4. Work one motif of Pattern #16. The center basting line runs through the center Cross Stitch (see graph, Figure 45).

5. Repeat on the right-hand side, working 2 rows of the pattern (see photo).

6. Turn under and stitch a ¾″ hem 14 threads away from the row of cross stitches.

7. Press the place mat.

*Figure 45*

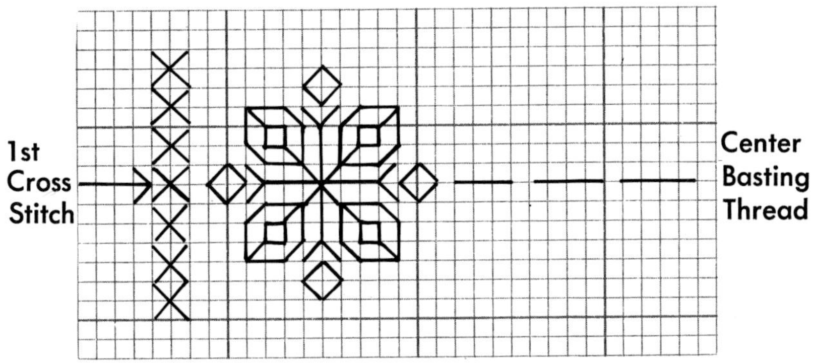

# *Tablecloth*    SEE COLOR PLATE 6.

## MATERIALS

1 piece of white even-weave linen, 22 threads per inch, 2″ larger
   all around than the finished size
Blue embroidery floss
Green embroidery floss
#22 tapestry needle

## INSTRUCTIONS

1. Follow steps 2 and 3A in "Starting a Project" on page 39.

2. On your sampler, practice Pattern #27 and back stitch, working the eye stitches in blue floss and the back stitches in the green. Use 3 strands of the embroidery floss (see closeup photo on Plate 6).

3. Work a blue Eye Stitch over the center point. The completed design is worked with a diamond shape (see photo). The easiest method of working this design is one row at a time, working one flower motif less on either side of each row. The green outside line of the diamond forms steps. (There will be 13 flower motifs in the center row, 1 flower motif in the final row.)

4. Count 128 threads from the final motif and work a row of Back stitches in green, over 2 threads, for the outside edge of the border. The border is 10 threads wide. Next, stitch the blue Eye stitches side by side inside the border, two threads away from the row of Back stitches. Finally, work another row of Back stitches 2 threads away from the Eye stitches. When working the border start in the center of each side with the center basting thread running through the middle of the Eye Stitch.

5. To complete, measure 3″ from the border and stitch a 1″ hem all around the cloth.

# *Floral Picture*

SEE COLOR PLATE 1.

## *14" x 14" inside frame*

## MATERIALS

1 piece of even-weave white linen, 15" x 15" (22 threads per inch)

3 skeins of black embroidery floss

#22 tapestry needle

1 bobbin of gold thread (DMC Fil d'Or à Broder)

## INSTRUCTIONS

1. Follow step 2 of "Starting a Project" on page 39.

2. Trace the flower design on page 152 onto a piece of tracing paper (Figure 46).

3. Follow the instructions on page 115 and transfer the design onto the linen.

4. On your sampler, practice Stem Stitch, couching satin stitch and Patterns #1, 8, 11, 24, 39, using 2 strands of embroidery floss.

5. In Stem Stitch, outline all the shapes excepting the body of the butterfly. (Do not work the veins of the leaves.)

6. Fill in the patterns as indicated by the numbers on the drawing. On Pattern #1, work the tiny Cross stitches, using 2 strands of gold thread. After the patterns are worked, stitch the veins of the leaves in Stem Stitch.

7. Stitch the body of the butterfly in Satin Stitch, using a double strand of the gold thread. Then outline the Satin Stitch in Couching. A tiny black cross is worked over 2 threads at the tip of each antenna.

8. Press the piece flat on the wrong side and frame as a picture or sew into a pillow.

Figure 46

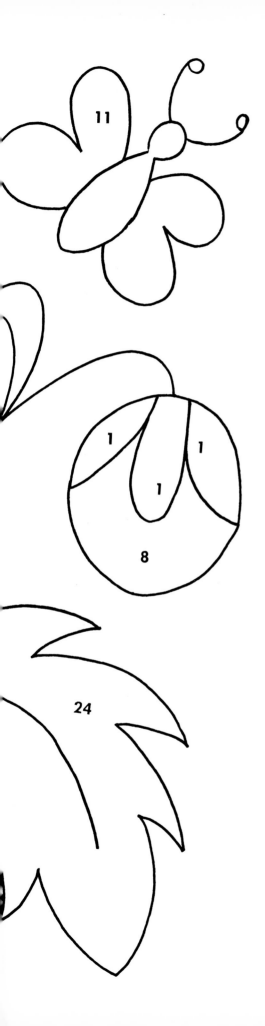

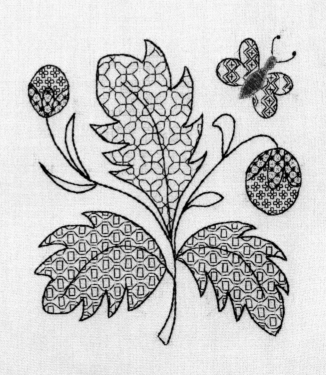

# *Butterfly Picture*   SEE COLOR PLATE 1.
## *14" x 10" inside frame*

## MATERIALS

1 piece of white even-weave linen, 16" x 12" (22 threads per inch)
2 skeins of black embroidery floss
1 bobbin of gold thread (DMC Fil d'Or à Broder)
#22 tapestry needle

## INSTRUCTIONS

1. Follow step 2 of "Starting a Project" on page 39. Fold the linen in half lengthwise and stitch a basting line down the fold (8" from the outside edge)

2. Trace the butterfly design on opposite page onto a piece of tracing paper (½ the butterfly is given—reverse the tracing paper to make a complete butterfly).

3. Using the drawing of the complete butterfly, transfer the design onto the linen (see instructions on page 115).

NOTE: The broken line down the center of the body should correspond to the basted center line on the linen.

4. On your sampler, practice Stem Stitch, Chain Stitch, Eye Stitch (using 2 strands of gold thread, and Patterns #1, 2, 5, 6, 8, 26, 29, and 41. In Stem Stitch outline all the shapes excepting the circles, which are outlined in small Chain stitches.

5. Fill in the patterns as indicated by the numbers on the drawing (Figure 47). In gold, work a single motif of Pattern #3 into the center of each circle. Press the piece flat on the wrong side and frame as a picture or sew into a pillow.

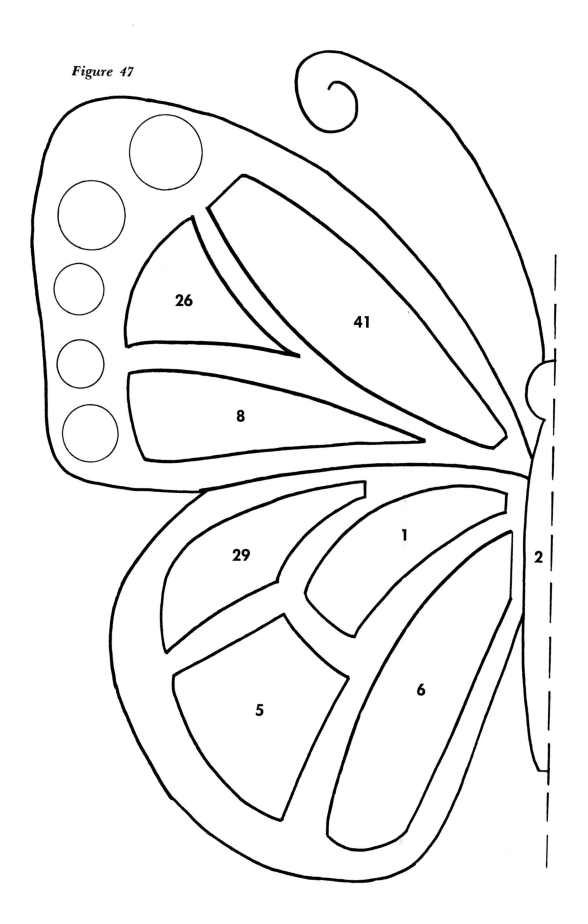

*Figure 47*

# Canvas Embroidery Pillow

*12" x 12"*         SEE COLOR PLATE 7.

## MATERIALS

1 piece of needlepoint canvas, 16" x 16" (14 threads per inch)
1 piece of black fabric (e.g., velvet) for pillow backing
1 pillow form, 14" x 14"
2 skeins of black embroidery floss
80 strands of pale-blue Persian-type tapestry wool
30 strands of black Persian-type tapestry wool (each strand approximately 33" long)
#22 tapestry needle

## INSTRUCTIONS

1. Bind the edges of the canvas with masking tape.

2. Draw a 14" square on the canvas, using a *waterproof* nylon-tipped marking pen (2" of extra canvas will be left all around).

3. Fold the canvas in half, and in half again, the opposite way. Draw a line down both creases. These are the centers.

4. The graph on page 108 shows how the pattern is worked (Figure 27).

NOTE: Persian wool is made up of 3 strands of wool. Separate the strands and use 2 strands (or one strand doubled).

5. Starting from the center point, work the first row of diamonds, being sure that when completed the center Cross Stitch worked in embroidery floss will be in the exact center of the pillow. The Back stitches and center Cross Stitch are worked using 2 strands of embroidery floss.

Each stitch is worked over 2 threads of the canvas. Completely fill the pillow with the pattern.

6. To make up the pillow:

   a. Using a damp cloth, press the embroidery right side down on a terry towel. If it is badly out of shape have the piece blocked professionally.

   b. Baste the embroidered piece and pillow back together, stitching as close to the embroidered edge as possible.

   c. Stitch around 3 sides and 1″ on either side of the fourth side. Trim the fabric ½″ and turn on to the right side. Square out the corners.

   d. Insert pillow form and slip-stitch the fourth side closed.

# *Embroidered Box*

SEE COLOR PLATE 3.

Embroidered work boxes and jewelry boxes have always been very popular and many old examples are still to be seen in museums around the world.


## COVERING A BOX

1. Using a cigar box or other similar box, cut out a paper pattern the exact size of the box plus 1″ all around for turnings.

2. Pin the paper pattern onto the linen and cut out each piece, basting a line to mark the exact size and shape of each piece.

3. I embroidered the lid of my box with Pattern #13, working the double Cross stitches in 2 strands of gold thread.

4. The four sides of the box were embroidered in Pattern #6. working the Straight stitches in 2 strands of gold thread.

5. Before covering the box with the finished embroidery, I padded it with a thin layer of cotton.

If you are not too good at sewing, as is the case with many accomplished embroiderers, ask a seamstress friend to help you cover the box.

# Embroidered Clothing

SEE COLOR PLATE 8.

Blackwork embroidery was used to adorn the clothing of both men and women of the sixteenth century. Today this is still one of the most pleasing ways to use the patterns.

There is no limit to how much blackwork you use to decorate clothing. Some people may prefer to cover an entire article with embroidery and others to enhance the collar and cuffs of a blouse with a pattern.

I used Patterns #8 and 29 to decorate the front of a simple blouse (see Plate 8).

Using a basic dress pattern, I embroidered the linen yoke of a dress for my daughter, using Pattern #23. I worked the embroidery before I made the dress.

# SUPPLIERS

* Indicates mail order available.

* The Yarn Depot, Inc.,
545 Sutter Street,
San Francisco, California 94100

Supplies a wide variety of yarns

* Merribe Co
4000 Saw Mill Run Boulevard,
Pittsburgh, Pennsylvania 15227

Fabric suitable for counted stitches

* The Needlewoman,
146-148 Regent Street,
London, WIR 6BA England

Even-weave linens; wide variety of
yarns

The Crafts Center,
Quaker Road,
Nantucket, Massachusetts 02554

Even-weave linens; stranded
embroidery floss; Persian yarn

* Boutique Margot,
26 West 54th., Street,
New York, New York 10019

Even-weave linens; wide variety of
yarns

* Art Needlework Treasure Trove,
P.O. Box 2440
New York, New York 10019

Even-weave linens; wide variety of
yarns and needlework equipment

Flying Colors,
9 South Lincoln,
Hinsdale, Illinois 60521

Even-weave linens; wide variety of
yarns

* Greek Island Ltd.,
215 East 49th Street
New York, New York 10017

Even-weave dresses and blouses